HOW TO DECIDE

WHAT TO DO NEXT

WHEN YOU'RE RETIRED

PUT YOUR TIME AND ENERGY
WHERE YOUR VALUES ARE

Jean Risley
the Retiree Assistant

Contents

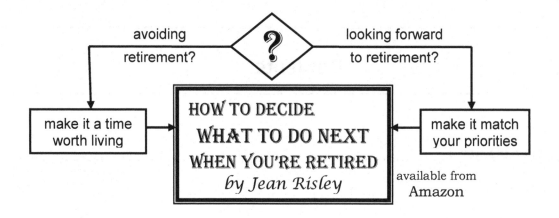

How to Use this Book

This book is meant to be a helper and not another taskmaster. It's meant to help you discover what you value and want to do, and then help you organize your time in the directions you want to go.

It's not meant to set up somebody else's standard that you ought to live up to. It is meant to help you live a life you feel good about, not in any way to make you feel inadequate or bad about yourself.

It's your retirement, and if you want to do nothing, make it one of your goals! Here "wasting time" means using your time for things you don't value. Resting, day dreaming, remembering, and simply being aren't "wasting time" when it's your choice to do them.

This book is a collection of tools that you can use (or not) when they're helpful to you. Pick the ones that are promising, and feel free to adapt them to your own needs and style. For example, if having specific times on your day plan is too detailed, just cross them out and use "morning" and "afternoon" instead. Your plan is whatever works for you.

As you work with these planning tools, it's a good time to talk your ideas over with your spouse or those closest to you. Knowing when your hopes and plans are uniquely your own and when they're shared with others in your life will clarify how you can make them a reality.

Feel free to make any copies of the worksheets that you need to write on, and fill them with your own thoughts. Don't be afraid to change your plans when you change your mind about them. It's your retirement, after all, so enjoy it your way.

1. Find Your Meaning

The feel of the first day of retirement can range from an ecstatic view of all the fun ahead, to a horrified "What am I going to do when I get out of bed today?" No matter where you fit on the spectrum of enthusiasm, the reality is that you have a multitude of possibilities ahead. How are you going to approach your choices?

In order to know which direction to step, it helps to know where you are and where you're going. The Chinese philosopher Lao-tzu said if we don't watch out, we will end up where we're headed. It's much easier to get there if you know where you want to be.

This section involves some questions to help define the path that will guide the choices you have to make. Who are you? What do you love? What matters to you? What brings you joy? Who do you want to be? How do you want to be remembered? These are not easy questions, but you are the only person who can answer them for yourself.

Who Are You?

We all have many different roles over a lifetime—child and adult, friend and rival, apprentice and expert, leader and follower, and perhaps even saint and scoundrel. Now the focus is on who you are when you're at your best.

Here are some questions to help you find and remember that person. As you think about these questions, you could also use a notebook to record your ideas.

What is unique about you that leads to your happiest times and your best performance?

_____

_____

What words or phrases best describe you as an individual?

_____

_____

Think about a particular time when you were doing something that felt particularly "natural" and "right." What were you doing, and what led to that feeling?

_____

_____

What are your signature strengths? What are the abilities, skills, and ways of thinking that you use when you are making your best contributions, doing your best work?

_____

_____

Find Your Meaning

Live the Stages

Getting Older

Identify Your Goals

Make Helpful Habits

Plan Your Days

Track Your Results

Practice Consistency

The person you just described gives you clues to your best and most authentic self. You'll be able to live most fully when you bring your authentic self to each new experience.

What do you love?

Inside each of us there is a small child who once believed that anything is possible. That child had dreams and fantasies about things that would be great fun to be and do and feel. Over the years, that child discovered that these dreams were simply unrealistic, and the child buried them deep inside. We need to meet that child again and explore those dreams to find out what we really love.

> When I was little I took ballet lessons, and I dreamed of being a famous dancer. Why? It was the Cold War, and I knew that dancers were highly respected in Russia. I hoped to be famous and respected enough on both sides to bring the two countries together.
>
> I turned to science rather than dance, but I still love the idea of bringing people to appreciate each other and work together. A fortune cookie I got just yesterday expresses this dream: "Let hatred turn into friendship because of your existence."

Of course not all dreams begin in childhood. A sudden moment of insight can happen at any time and any age. Unfortunately, when we're older and more practical, we may quickly turn away from the vision of what might be because it seems so "unrealistic."

Why do you need to find these lost dreams? They're the key to your love for your vocation and interests, and those old feelings can become an important component of your future happiness.

How can you recover these dreams? Here are two exercises that might help you find them:
o   What attracted or fascinated you when you were a child? What did you love to do or daydream about?

_____

_____

o   What might you have been or done if you had all the best luck when you were growing up? supportive parents? the best education? unlimited resources? access to any opportunities? What could you have been?

_____

_____

How do you distill these dreams to find their core elements? Once you've identified a dream, you need to figure out what it is about the dream that really appeals to you. For example, if your dream is to have a luxurious house on the top of a mountain, you need to decide what matters—having the money to buy a place like that, living in a fancy place, having a great view, or being in the mountains. What you love in the dream could be having money, living comfortably, enjoying beautiful scenery, or the mountains themselves. As you look at your dream closely, you should be able to isolate which parts of it still speak to your longings today.

How do you bring your loves into your present life? Here are some ideas to help you think about it:

o Think of 20 or more things you still like to do, then choose the top half dozen.

_____

_____

o Think about your ideal situation and environment. What would be included in it?

_____

_____

o Think about your ideal day. What would you like to be part of it?

_____

_____

Think about the different elements of your days. Which people, places, and things are necessary for you, which are desirable, and which are optional?

element	necessary	desirable	optional
Who?			
Where?			
What?			

Alice's Own Wonderland

I knew Alice from the time we were raising toddlers together. She was an English teacher, but she managed to find totally unexpected jobs, like teaching high school equivalency in a women's prison. It wasn't until near retirement age that she found her true calling as an actor in community theater.

Like Robin Williams, her conversation was always full of creative humor. Now her beautifully pointed style lets her charm the audience in shows like Nunsense, the Cemetery Club, Steel Magnolias, and most recently as Dr. Ruth. Her challenge at present is that her age leads to audition calls for grandmotherly roles, while her acting style fits high intensity characters.

What Matters to You?

It shouldn't be hard to identify what you care about. It's there in the way you react about an open question like "How's it going?" or a general comment like "The

Find Your Meaning
Live the Stages
Getting Older
Identify Your Goals
Make Helpful Habits
Plan Your Days
Track Your Results
Practice Consistency

world's a mess." It can be concern for a situation you just can't ignore. It can be an ache for an experience you never got the chance to have. It can be an injustice you see that just drives you crazy. It can be something you see that no one wants to fix or that you just know needs to be done.

Do you have a message that you want to share with the world? Have you found an insight that folks around you don't seem to have discovered? Is there a group of people that you long to help or encourage? One study of successful people showed that they tend to have a personal message that's part of everything they do. They're present and engaged because their message is part of their fundamental character.

What you care about is at the heart of your purpose. It provides you inspiration and the motivation to keep going, to keep moving as best you can, toward your life's most important achievements. None of us can completely solve the world's problems, but we need to know that our piece of the work is real and that we are making a significant contribution for good. Our passions are our fuel for the journey.

What Brings You Joy?

When we're working on something we believe in and using our best strengths and abilities, we'll find joy coming out of our work, because this work creates joy and energy in itself. When we spend our time on what we do well and enjoy, our lives not only have meaning but we feel truly alive.

But life, and especially life in retirement, is not only about working toward our purpose in life. To keep doing what we care about also means to be in it for the long haul. It means preserving our energy and enthusiasm as well as using them. It requires regular rest and relaxation. We need to rest from time to time to start again with renewed strength.

In order to keep going, you need to know what kinds of things bring you back to life and energy. Where do you find your rest? What gives you joy and refreshment?

Your sources of refreshment are completely unique for you. Some folks are energized by bright lights and lively music, while others find that solitude and quiet refills their reservoir. Some find joy with grandchildren, actual or borrowed, while others find comfort just sitting with an old friend. Some are refreshed by using their hands, doing crafts like knitting or working with wood.

In order to be resilient, to bounce back from time of effort or struggle, you need to know for yourself what brings you peace. Some love classical music. Others love just being outdoors with the sun shining. I love just being in the water, not necessarily swimming, but just feeling held and lifted by the water. I love being on the water, too, so my perfect extended care facility would have a dock and a pontoon boat.

There are so many choices and possibilities that you might want to explore and experiment to see what works for you. Where do you find your peace?

_____

_____

Who Do You Want To Be?

How do you like to think of yourself? Do you want to be:
- o   the kind of person your dog thinks you are
- o   the person your favorite grandchild thinks you are
- o   Mother Teresa for a group of people whose needs touch your heart
- o   a great fisherman, hiker, finance person, volunteer, caregiver, ...
- o   a fighter for truth and justice
- o   someone who makes people feel happy, safe, confident, inspired, ...
- o   mentor for people who want to ...

What is your favorite image of yourself?

_____

_____

To make it real, you might want to write a description of your retirement life. It doesn't need to be long, but it should include
- o   your activities and interests
- o   your health
- o   your home
- o   your relationships
- o   things you want to do

When you have your life description on paper, it's easier to look at it from the outside to see if it really reflects the way you want to live. Living with your description for a few days or building it slowly over time, making changes as they occur to you, can help you come to a vision that feels comfortable.

_____

_____

_____

_____

Even in retirement, productivity matters. Most of us won't be happy if we don't produce in some way. This life is not entirely rest, even when we're not going out to work. Yes, we must rest, but only long enough to gather strength to get back to doing what matters. Time is the greatest and rarest of commodities. At this stage of life, we should all be intimately aware of how precious each day is and know better than to waste a second.

Find Your Meaning

Live the Stages

Getting Older

Identify Your Goals

Make Helpful Habits

Plan Your Days

Track Your Results

Practice Consistency

How Do You Want to be Remembered?

Think about your obituary. Beyond the basics, what would you like it to say about you?

_____

_____

Think of all the different roles you are filling and write down a short statement of how you would like to be described in each role. How would you like the important people in your life to remember you and talk about you?

_____

_____

_____

_____

_____

There may be some folks you've known whose memory of you is not very favorable. There's no time like the present to repair any broken relationships in the past or present. Whether it takes reaching out to show you care, apologizing and making amends for some fault (real or imagined), or unraveling and correcting a misunderstanding, today is always a good time to start to leave a happier memory.

Be Yourself

The cliché is actually true: you are unique. You are the only one with your combination of talents, passions, perspectives, and experiences. Others may be able to give you good advice and even insights about yourself, but ultimately you are the one who knows what you can do. You are the only one who can succeed at being yourself.

At retirement age, we've been around long enough to know that we can't please everyone, even if we wanted to. Now it's time to be ourselves. Some people will like us and some will not. Some will show good taste, and the others we don't need to worry about. It's reasonable to accept help and feedback from others, but don't let others define the person you want to be.

Our time is valuable, and we need to use it for what's important to us. I don't mean that we should be rude or uncaring, but there's no point in wasting time worrying about what others will think of us. If you want to wear purple, wear purple!

Why Have a Personal Purpose Statement?

A personal purpose statement captures who you are and what you're here on earth for. It's a brief description of what you want to focus on, what you want to accomplish and who you want to become over the next few years. It's a way to focus your energy, actions, behaviors, and decisions towards the things that are most important to you.

A personal purpose statement answers questions like these:

o What do I want from my life?
o What do I believe in?
o What do I value?
o What are my talents?
o What do I hope to accomplish?
o How do I want to be remembered?
o Anything else I might want to include.

Writing a personal purpose statement forces you to think deeply about your life, to clarify the purpose of your life, and to identify what's really important to you. It forces you to clarify and express your deepest values and aspirations. It anchors your values and purpose firmly in your mind so they become an active part of you, rather than something you only think about from time to time. When you integrate your personal purpose statement into your weekly planning, it gives you a way to keep your purpose constantly in mind.

Your purpose statement also has a particular value when you're over tired, over stressed, or otherwise not at your best. It provides you with a foundation, a solid ground you can come back to. When you have trouble holding things together, it can remind you of who you are and what you consider truly important.

Create Your Personal Purpose Statement

Begin by thinking about people either in history or in your own life that you admire. What qualities do those people have that you would like to emulate. What do you value in them? their character? their values? their achievements? their personality? or simply the way they live their lives? Think about the specific reasons you admire these people and make a list of those qualities.

_____

_____

Imagine your ideal self, who it is you want to become. Picture the details of your accomplishments, your personality, or any future you'd like to experience. This ideal should reflect your core values and your understanding of living with integrity. Think about specific actions, behaviors, habits and qualities that would have a significant positive impact on your life over the next few years. Describe this ideal self.

_____

_____

Identify your past successes. Spend some time finding four or five examples of personal success in recent years. These successes could be at work, in your

Find Your Meaning

Live the Stages

Getting Older

Identify Your Goals

Make Helpful Habits

Plan Your Days

Track Your Results

Practice Consistency

community, at home, or wherever. Try to identify whether there's a common theme — or themes — in your examples. What themes do you find?

_____

_____

_____

Identify your core values. Create a list of attributes that you believe identify who you are and what your priorities are. Then narrow the list of values to the five or six most important. From those, choose the single value that is most important to you.

_____

_____

_____

What are the talents and skills you have that are most important to you and that you actually enjoy using? Make a list of all of your personal and professional talents, aptitudes, and skills — even those you may take for granted. When you have the full list, identify the skills you enjoy most or find most fulfilling.

_____

_____

_____

We tend to go about our lives without considering the purpose for our essential being and how we want to direct that purpose. Think about the part you play in each of the roles in your life and how you would like to function in each of these roles. Your roles may be in your profession, your family, your community, or other areas in your life. Try to capture your purpose in each of these roles. In each role, what is the most important way you want to express yourself?

_____

_____

_____

Identify your potential contributions. Make a list of the ways you could make a difference. In an ideal situation, what kinds of contributions could you make to the world in general, your family, your friends, and your community?

_____

_____

_____

In the end, your actual purpose statement could be no longer than a paragraph. Try to capture the most important ideas from your goals, your beliefs and your values. Keep it simple, clear, and brief. The most succinct purpose statements tend to be 3 to 5 sentences long. Let your feelings show, because including an emotional side in your purpose statement gives it passion and makes it more compelling, inspiring, and energizing.

One way to craft a purpose statement is to use a simple form like "I am {identity} who can {capabilities} and intends to {direction}." You can use the worksheet to collect your thoughts, and then combine and massage them into a final statement.

Personal Purpose Worksheet

Identity

I am a _____ (who I am, who I want to be).

I have _____ (past successes).

I am a person of _____ (qualities, character traits).

I value _____ (core values).

Capabilities

I am known for _____ (signature strengths).

I am good at _____ (talents, skills).

I usually _____ (behaviors, habits).

Direction

I care deeply about _____ (passion).

I was created to _____ (calling).

I hope to _____ (purpose).

I want to be remembered as _____ (legacy).

It is important that _____ (concerns).

Now take the most important and most distinctive ideas from these statements and distill them into a single concise paragraph that represents you. Move things around until you feel the words express where you want to go.

_____

_____

_____

_____

_____

_____

_____

_____

_____

_____

Find Your Meaning

Live the Stages

Getting Older

Identify Your Goals

Make Helpful Habits

Plan Your Days

Track Your Results

Practice Consistency

2. Live One Stage at a Time

There are several ways of describing the stages of retirement, but simplest is a division into three stages based on physical requirements and limitations. The activities in each stage may be different, but there is a continuous thread in each of the areas of life that flows through the stages.

In each stage it's critical to keep engaging with what we love while making the accommodations that we need. There's a difference between simply staying alive and having a life worth living. In order to keep what's important to us, we need to plan for the transitions that increasing limitations will require.

There are three stages of retirement based on our physical, mental, and financial resources. The first stage is active retirement, sometimes referred to as the *go-go* period. In this period we have almost all the energy we used to have, and we have all our time to do the things we've always wanted to do. The second stage begins slowing down, sometimes called the *slo-go* period. This is a time when health care absorbs some of our time, and physical issues limit our choice of activities. In the third stage, sometimes called the *no-go* period, our ability to get around is limited, and we may need more care from others.

Which Aspects of Life Change?

In each of the stages you'll need to consider each of the areas of your life:
o environment – where you'll live, how you'll eat, how you'll get around
o health – exercise, medications, therapies, hospitalization, etc.
o interests – work (paid or volunteer), hobbies, sports, learning
o happiness – fun, entertainment, recreation, travel
o relationships – family, friends, neighbors, community
o spirituality – faith, religious exploration, meditation

You're the person who knows what is important to you in each area and what can be scaled back. For example, you may want to move to an easier-to-maintain home in a lower cost area, or nearer family, or in a more congenial climate, or near particular medical facilities. One strategy doesn't work for everyone, and you need to know what matters to you in order to make choices.

In each stage of retirement, you should be thinking ahead, making plans to adapt the activities you love to the next stage. A sailor might consider moving to a motor boat or a time-share on the harbor. A skier might consider whether local smaller slopes would satisfy the longing for the mountains, or whether taking up golf would be a better choice. Thinking ahead might also help us savor the things we love to do, while we are still able to do them.

Active Retirement

In the active *go-go* stage of retirement, we're usually physically and mentally

Find Your Meaning

Live the Stages

Getting Older

Identify Your Goals

Make Helpful Habits

Plan Your Days

Track Your Results

Practice Consistency

capable of an active lifestyle. Within our budget, we're capable of doing almost anything we can afford, because we have enough time for the activities we enjoy.

We also have some time for some things that look like work, whether paid or not. If we love what we used to do for a living, we might find a way to continue on a smaller scale, perhaps with fewer responsibilities. If we want or need more money, there are some unglamorous possibilities. Even greeting at the discount store or bagging at the grocery store can provide social interactions as well as an active environment with a little cash included.

Active retirement is a very free time, for many of us a period of travel, hobbies and adventure. In deciding how to spend our time and money, it helps to know approximately how much we have to live on. Then we can allocate our resources and balance them across our activities in all the areas of life.

Slowing Down

The second *slo-go* stage begins when we find we no longer have the energy and stamina to fill our days with activity. We may still be able to do some or most of our favorite activities, but we just can't put many in a day. Some activities, though, have become difficult. We can't walk as far or as fast, we can't climb stairs as easily, and we need more time to do almost anything. We get tired more easily and need more rest.

This is a time to conserve energy so we can spend it where it counts. We may downsize and reduce maintenance tasks to focus on the things we love. We may need to pay for support services to cover or assist with some activities. We may step back from some activities, like driving at night, where we don't feel confident or reliable. We may need to devote more time to medical issues and health maintenance. With lower energy, this tends to be a stage for spending time with family and friends, a time marked by social activities, recreation, and relaxation.

Living in Place

It can be hard to predict what our level of mobility, motivation and health will be in our later *no-go* retirement years. It's a time of winding down, when most of our time is spent at home, whether this is our usual place or a residential community. We continue to have less energy and less physical ability. We need more medical care, and we may be restricted to home because of declining health. We may need physical, emotional, or financial support, or simply someone we trust to defend our interests. We will still want to enjoy some of our long-term interests, our memories, and the companionship of family and friends.

Think through Your Choices

As you consider your options, you might want to ask yourself:
> What do I think I will be able to handle as I get older?
> What aspects of daily life matter to me most?
> What do I need to survive?
> What do I need to feel alive?
> What can I live without?

What kind of help can I live with?

What kind of help can I afford?

A Tale of Two Sisters

My mother was a planner, and she had moved from place to place with my father's jobs. She was a corporate wife, active in organizations in town and supporting father's business. When father's retirement came, she decided that the house and yard were too much work, and so they moved to a spacious apartment with a great view.

Her sister was an artist, having a career as a draftsman and marrying late in life to a congenial retired steelworker. She lived on the side of a mountain in the Pennsylvania Dutch country, a rural area where good health care and just about everything else were about an hour away. Like my mother, my aunt believed that as long as they were a couple, if anything happened to either of them, they could take care of each other.

Mother knew where they would live "when the time comes," a community with apartments, assisted living, and nursing care for all stages of independence. The only problem was that she didn't want to make that move until it was necessary. The complex required that both of the couple be in good health, and they delayed the move until my father almost didn't make the requirement.

My aunt had no plans and no local facilities other than end-of-life nursing care. When her husband passed away, she could barely cope, with rides and groceries from people at her church. When she found herself in the hospital, they wouldn't discharge her unless she had somewhere to go and someone who could take care of her. She had no children, and fortunately she was willing to come to a similar community (with an indoor pool for the swimming she loved) near where I was living.

Both sisters found their way to communities that could serve the needs of their different life stages, moving back and forth between apartment, assisted living, and nursing care as their health and capabilities required. But both came close to being in a situation where their future passed out of their control.

Use the Life Stage Planning Worksheet to place the elements of your life that matter most to you into the three different stages.

It is particularly important to make sure that family members or others that you trust to make decisions on your behalf are aware of your thoughts and plans for the different stages.

Find Your Meaning

Live the Stages

Getting Older

Identify Your Goals

Make Helpful Habits

Plan Your Days

Track Your Results

Practice Consistency

Life Stage Planning Sample

activity	active period	slower period	in place period
environment	house / apartment	home possible long term houseguest	assisted living or (modified) home extended care facility
home care	minimalist doing supplementary services	cleaning service yard service	outside services or provided in package
food	as can meals out	prepared or meals on wheels grocery delivery	outside services or provided in package
clothing	regular	minimal	leftovers
health	insurance and copays special services	insurance and copays special services	insurance and copays special services
transportation	driving	some driving paid drivers	paid drivers bus services
shopping	local stores Internet	Internet catalog	Internet catalog
vocation			
interests			
happiness	day trip outings travel with family or friends	day trip outings travel with family as possible	group outings travel to events with groups
family	weekly grandkid time holiday gatherings	grandkid visits holiday gatherings	holiday visits
relationships	activities with friends	visits with friends	neighbor interactions
spirituality			

Life Stage Planning Worksheet

activity	active period	slower period	in place period
environment			
home care			
food			
clothing			
health			
transportation			
shopping			
vocation			
interests			
happiness			
family			
relationships			
spirituality			

Find Your Meaning	Live the Stages	Getting Older	Identify Your Goals	Make Helpful Habits	Plan Your Days	Track Your Results	Practice Consistency

3. Getting Old Is Not for Wimps (but it beats the alternative)

Find Your Meaning

Live the Stages

Getting Older

Identify Your Goals

Make Helpful Habits

Plan Your Days

Track Your Results

Practice Consistency

Discovering that we're getting older is almost always unexpected. We may see ourselves in a passing mirror or find that something we always did easily is suddenly harder. We may pretend that this warning sign didn't happen and be caught by a bad surprise, like an accident or a fall. Sooner or later, though, we come to realize that we are not getting any younger.

This book is about taking control of our lives as we age. We have choices, and a little planning can keep us from being surprised by the effects of age that we can't avoid. We each have different priorities and preferences, and my goal is to help each of us make our own choices rather than let time or circumstances make them for us.

Aging presents us with many different kinds of challenges. We want to do our best with what we still have, but we face lots of unexpected twists and turns. We are changing and the world around us is changing.

Reduced Physical Capabilities

We lose different abilities at different rates, but we all deteriorate over time. We discover that we tire more easily, take longer to do things, have trouble getting around, lose our balance, and find obstacles where none had been before.

Reduced Mental Capabilities

Some mental losses we notice easily: we forget names, reach for words, and have trouble multitasking. We call these senior moments. More problematic are the times when we are losing it, but don't notice that it's happening.

Increasing Complexity

Society around us is constantly changing, both technologically and culturally. Doing things that used to be simple has become more complicated. We encounter more different kinds of people, with different backgrounds and behaviors.

Outside Expectations

Those around us, friends and strangers, have expectations that are often hard to understand, much less satisfy. We sometimes feel lost and confused when it seems that our familiar world has become a foreign country.

Loss of Control

We risk losing control of our lives and ourselves. Others, some well-meaning and some not, offer to help us by taking care of us.

What does losing control feel like? When I had knee replacements and went to a hospital for rehabilitation, it was decided that I had balance problems and was at risk for falling. I had a yellow bracelet that meant I couldn't walk alone. I needed to call for help to go to the bathroom, wash, dress, get a pillow or blanket, or walk in the hall. My bed had a siren that sounded if I tried to get out of bed. The physical therapist said I should walk often, but each time I had to wait for an attendant to have time to be my babysitter. I had to become very polite so the attendants would be in a good mood when I called.

There's no question that aging is scary. We're used to being capable, and the side-effects of getting older undermine that. In our lives so far, things have usually gotten better as we go, and we have gotten used to that sense of good progress. Now we need to face and deal with the reality that things will mostly be getting worse, perhaps quickly or perhaps slowly, but inevitably. Do we have the courage to age well, to accept what we can't change, and to make lemonade out of the limitations that age throws at us?

We're probably the first generation in history that was led to believe that we could live forever, and that things would keep getting better. Now we're faced with the hard reality that we're not exempt from aging, just like all the generations before us. We can try to ignore it. We can hide from it. Or we can accept it and take the chance to make it into something positive.

Making Lemonade

We each have the chance to make the best we can out of the circumstances we find ourselves in. We will each get different lemons, some physical, some mental, some financial, and some relational. We don't want to dwell on the negatives and get depressed about them. We do need to think about them just enough to make plans to deal with them, and then to get back to the business of enjoying life each day.

It's critically important to know what you want and how you want to live through the different stages of aging. Some things will matter to you and some will not. The things that matter to you will be different from the things that matter to me. Only you, with the counsel and support of those close to you, know what you want and need.

If we want to stay in control, we need to preserve both the appearance of competence and the reality of competent control. The tools in this workbook can give you a framework for thinking about your future—what you want it to include, the things you can do to make it happen, and ways to take into account the physical changes that can't be avoided. You may want to write down ideas as they occur to you. How you build your future is, and can stay, in your own hands.

Yes, I know that it's not fun to think about the negative possibilities. The point of thinking about them, of making some level of contingency plans, and then putting those plans away until they're needed is that if and when the negative happens, you'll be ready. Your choices will be in place when they're needed.

I've told the following story of my friend Bernard a number of times, and some folks don't like it very much. After all, Bernard had terrible limitations, and none of us want to be in his situation. But knowing his story gives me great hope, because if he could make such a rich life with all his challenges, surely the rest of us can do at least as well. You can skip it, or you can see a story of real life courage:

Living Well with Extreme Disability

When I first met him, Bernard was in the late stages of ALS, Lou Gehrig's disease. He was almost totally paralyzed, on life support, and only able to move his eyes and one eyebrow. His hospital bed was in the dining area of the small ranch house where he lived with his second wife. He communicated by moving his eyebrow to choose letters from an alphabet board. Within these limits, Bernard managed to live a rich life.

- He was interested in history. He liked to watch history shows on TV and listen to biographies through books on tape.
- He loved spring and summer when he could listen through the open windows to the children playing in the playground behind the house.
- He had a motorized wheelchair with full life support, and his wife was able to rent a handicapped van to go on outings.
- When they decided to redo the kitchen, he was involved in all the details of planning and construction.
- He wanted to take his teenaged sons to a Knicks game at Madison Square Garden, and they all got to sit down in front near the players.
- He gave a barbecue birthday party where we could all meet his friends and extended family.
- He wanted a dog, so they got a gentle older female Rottweiler. He named her Otis after Otis Redding, even though she was a girl. Otis was very protective of him, but also a charming mooch who saved treats she didn't want to eat right away.
- He was troubled by his early involvement with voodoo and asked to be baptized. Even though he couldn't swallow, his nurse figured a way for him to take communion.
- One summer day he came to church to see the children's gathering and singing at Vacation Bible School.
- He was very interested in everything that went on around him. At first my husband would wait for me in the car when we visited. After my husband came to the baptism, he would ask where my husband was if I came to visit alone.

Bernard has become my role model for the way it's possible to live a rich, full life, even with incapacitating limitations and in the knowledge that the physical situation would get worse.

Find Your Meaning

Live the Stages

Getting Older

Identify Your Goals

Make Helpful Habits

Plan Your Days

Track Your Results

Practice Consistency

4. Identify Goals and Directions

In life, you won't go far unless you know where the goalposts are.
— fortune cookie

Once you've decided where you want to go, it's time to pull out the maps and choose the way you want to get there. As retirees, we may not want to go the fastest way, but to plan the trip to include nice scenery and interesting stops along the way. Our goals should reflect the way we want to go through the next stage of our lives and the things we want to do and enjoy while we're there.

Why Be Specific about Our Goals?

It helps to write down the main things we want to accomplish, the major goals that we hope to achieve. When we physically have our goals in front us every day, we naturally begin to think about them much more. As we spend time thinking about what we want to do, we tend to gravitate in the right direction.

Sherlock Holmes once compared our minds to an attic crammed full of stuff. Since we've accumulated lots of memories and experiences over the years, it can be harder to keep in mind the things that are current or truly important. Having our goals on paper and looking at them regularly can keep us on track, especially if getting to the goal will take some time.

How Do Goals Work?

Goals are a way of organizing all the different activities you need to do to get something done. Some activities depend on having finished some other activity first, while others just need to be finished sometime before the end. Usually a significant goal takes more activities and details than you can keep in mind at once, so a way of organizing them keeps you from losing a critical piece.

Goals need to be specific, not least because you need to know when you've gotten there. They need to be measurable in some way, so that you can tell if you're making progress, or not. "Get in shape" is not as effective a goal as "Do workouts 5 times a week."

Goals should come with a list of activities that, once completed, will actually achieve the goal. If your goal is regular workouts, specific activities might include starting with basics 3 times a week, adding strength training, increasing the length of workouts, and building up to a particular number of hours per week. Small, incremental actions turn into real steps making progress toward the goal.

Activities should be small, measurable, and under your own control. If an activity takes more than a few hours, it should be divided into several smaller chunks. You should be able to see clearly when an activity is done, so that "do yard work" is not as effective as "rake the leaves in the front yard." An activity also should be

Find Your Meaning

Live the Stages

Getting Older

Identify Your Goals

Make Helpful Habits

Plan Your Days

Track Your Results

Practice Consistency

23

something you can actually do. For example, you can't guarantee that you can "recruit 2 volunteers," but you can "make 5 calls to potential volunteers."

When you create your goals, make sure they're things you really care about making happen. If you don't really care, you won't make the time to make progress.

Keep focused and do whatever you need to do to keep your goals in mind. Make a sign, put a reminder on the mirror, keep a list on the breakfast table or the fridge, or scatter sticky notes in the kitchen. Tell people what you're working on and encourage them to ask you how it's going. Find people who will help you, encourage you and, when necessary, hold your feet to the fire.

Make sure there are rewards coming, not just when the goal is reached, but at other points along the way. Have a way to gauge your progress and celebrate your successes along the way.

What Aspects of Life Should Goals Cover?

Some folks recommend having 7 to 10 goals active at any one time. I find that having one goal at a time in each major area of life is about as many as I can work on at one time. Some of the activities toward the goals can be built into daily routines, while others will go onto your active to-do list.

Having goals in each area makes it possible to develop a balance over days and weeks. We want to maintain our health at the same time that we want to pursue our interests and have time with our families. Having explicit goals and activities in each area lets us make progress in each without sacrificing one to the other.

In the following sections we'll consider building goals in the life areas of vocation and interests, health and fitness, happiness, relationships, living environment, and spirituality. At the end you will find a pattern for building your own specific goals.

Some of us come to the end of a long career working in a particular field and have had enough of that field for a lifetime. Others of us come to the end of our career still enjoying the work, or at least some part of it, that we've been doing. As we come into retirement, we may or may not want to have anything to do with our past work life.

The good news is that in retirement the things we do with our time are separated from the way we make a living. For many reasons, it's not likely that we can make anywhere near the money we were making in mid-career.

The bad news, of course, is that whatever we decide to do for money is not going to bring in very much of it. A side effect of this is that if making a lot of money was critical to our identity or self-image, it's time to build a new one.

On the positive side, in retirement our vocations and avocations now fit into a single bucket: the collection of things we do that are meaningful to us and use the strengths we most enjoy. We no longer have to get out into the business world to do something because someone else tells us to. We now have the choice to do what we find interesting and rewarding, and to go where we need to go to do it.

Some of the things we do in our interest areas will support the work of our personal purpose, and others will provide us with joy, refreshment, and renewed energy. In both cases our involvement will be purposeful, with goals and activities that we can build into our plans.

What Do You Include in Your Vocation and Interests?

Activities in this area include paid work, volunteer work, hobbies, and anything else you might like to do.

Most of us have things we've always wanted to do or try. Why not list them and start tackling them? You can put anything on the list that sounds like fun to you.

_____

_____

_____

How about things you've always wondered about or classes with interesting titles that you never had the time to take? You can explore any of hundreds of fascinating disciplines. Write down some likely examples:

_____

_____

Find Your Meaning

Live the Stages

Getting Older

Identify Your Goals

Make Helpful Habits

Plan Your Days

Track Your Results

Practice Consistency

What about your creative side? You might discover talents you never knew were there and create something that is uniquely yours. Art, music, dance, writing, and all kinds of handicrafts are there waiting to be tried. The process is easy: explore, learn, practice, repeat. What would you like to try?

_____

_____

Are you interested in long-term or self-directed projects like creating a family tree, making a scrapbook, or designing a garden? The possibilities are endless. Be sure to note your individual project ideas and think about the resources, contacts, supplies, tasks and steps to help you stay organized.

_____

_____

What goals might you want to establish in your own areas of interest? Maybe:
o   learn a new skill or craft?
o   grow an existing hobby or try a new one?
o   use your old job skills for money or charity?
o   get to know a new culture or ethnic group?
o   find your family's roots and history?
o   have time to really follow your favorite sport?
o   learn to appreciate a new flavor of music or art?
What are some goals that you find particularly appealing?

_____

_____

_____

_____

_____

_____

How will you recognize success in your vocation and interests?

I am using my time to pursue several interests.
I love what I am doing.
I feel I am having a positive impact on the world.
I enjoy the recognition of those around me.
I have a hobby or hobbies I enjoy doing.
I enjoy pursuing my hobbies with other like-minded people.
I am involved in a charity where I use my talents for a good cause.

We all know that good health and fitness will give us more days to live and more ability to enjoy the days we have. Why isn't that enough motivation to have us doing the right things all the time? Organizing to help our behaviors match our intentions can bring the two closer together.

Eat Right

We all know it's important to eat properly. We've been told so for many years. We also know that sometimes we do and sometimes we don't do what we're supposed to. The problem with following a very strict diet or regimen is that when we fall off the wagon, we tend to give up, get depressed, and do the opposite of what we're supposed to. If you're one of those folks who are blessed with the desire and ability to eat healthy, you can skip this section.

Food choices are not one size fits all, even though many experts sound as if this were true. As a diabetic, my recommended meal pattern is five small meals a day rather than the usual three. Drinking lots of water is almost always good, except when there's a urinary issue. For most folks, a significant amount of fiber is a good thing, except if there are intestinal problems of a particular kind. Only your doctor or nutritionist can say what's right for you.

Once you understand your nutritional needs based on your unique situation, it's time to take things seriously and follow the instructions.

When you know what your eating/nutritional plan should be, you can look at your current practices and plan to make changes. Like any other goal, those changes need to be thought through carefully so they're behaviors you can get used to, live with, and turn into good habits you don't even think about.

Especially with food goals, you need to look carefully at the reasons behind your current misbehaviors. If you tend to indulge at a particular time of day, you may want to plan a distracting activity. If you're an emotional eater, eating to cheer up or feel less sad, you may want to find other small ways to add cheer to your day. If necessary, keeping a food diary can help you spot the places and reasons you get off track.

Find out from your professionals what kind of supplements you should be taking. Vitamin C and D, for example, both have positive benefits and are not as plentiful in our diets as they might be. Of course you should always verify with your doctor that any good ideas you hear, especially from vendors, are actually good for you.

Packing and carrying along snacks that are healthy for you helps keep up your energy wherever you are, and also keeps you from reaching out for whatever is handy at the time.

Find Your Meaning

Live the Stages

Getting Older

Identify Your Goals

Make Helpful Habits

Plan Your Days

Track Your Results

Practice Consistency

What kind of goals do you think might help you with your food and nutrition?

_____

_____

_____

Get Fit

There is no question that getting moving and keeping moving is a good thing. This is one place where "use it or lose it" is frighteningly true. If we don't get out of the chair or off the couch, we will lose the ability to get up at all. And then things just go downhill from there.

We need to move every day to keep the ability to move. We need to walk often, around the house, around the yard, around the block, down the hall and back, a little at a time, several times each day. When we've been sitting for a while, we need to stretch our legs just to keep our blood circulating. Back when we were working, there were lots of reasons to move—get coffee, ask a question, deliver some papers, chat with a friend. Now motion is something we need to do for ourselves, often by ourselves, at least every hour.

Real exercise has also got to be part of our daily routine. An exercise period in the morning actually gives you a burst of energy as your body gets going, and it also stimulates your mind and senses. Taking even a short walk outdoors or at the mall really is good for the heart. Walking from a farther away parking space or taking a few extra trips up stairs can add exercise unobtrusively.

To start a new exercise habit, pick a time when you'll be able to exercise consistently, like first thing in the morning. Build some cues into your day that remind you to get moving, like putting out exercise clothes where you'll see them. Make your exercise plan into a formal goal to maximize the chance of having a program you'll stick to.

Another key to making exercise part of your life is being prepared for inevitable resistance (it happens to everyone). Plan your strategy to head off excuses before they distract you. Make exercise a habit, like brushing your teeth, that you don't have to think about because you just do it when the time comes.

Finally, give yourself a little reward every time you finish exercising. The idea is that this will trick your brain into associating the rush of pleasure that comes from a treat with exercise. Build your own motivation with milestones and rewards that matter to you.

What kind of goals do you think might help you with your fitness?

_____

_____

_____

Exercise Your Mind

Your body needs to keep moving to keep working, and the same is true of your mind. Many of our favorite pastimes are passive, particularly movies and television. There we are passive consumers of experience and information, simply receivers and not doers. Taking a day or two a week to do without video is healthy, and there are other, more active alternatives that can be just as entertaining.

Reading a book instead of watching a show is an active exercise for your brain, since your mind has to actively construct mental images while you're reading. Doing puzzles of different kinds gets your brain moving as well, and there are games that exercise particular areas like memory and reasoning. Having a craft hobby where you design the product you are creating is great for using many parts of your brain. Games, even video games, keep your brain engaged, and the extra bonus in traditional games in the interaction with the other players.

When you are interacting with others regularly, you can pick up some of their habits and ways of thinking. To expand your mind, try spending time hanging out with people who are smarter than you are. In particular, spend some time in conversation with people who disagree with you. Friendly discussion across differences can clarify why you think what you think, or possibly expand your perspective to let you see how you were wrong.

The ultimate way to keep your mind going and growing is to keep learning new things. This doesn't mean to follow the latest fads, but to explore things you haven't done or thought about before. There are introductions (supposedly for dummies but actually for anybody who doesn't already know what they have to say) for everything from plumbing to history to physics to get you started. Once you find a thread that appeals to you, you can follow it as far and as deep as you like.

What kind of goals would help you keep and grow your mind?

_____

_____

_____

Get Enough Rest

We need more rest as we get older, and we come from a culture where most of us haven't been getting enough rest. There are prejudices against those who aren't always busy, and we may have felt guilty whenever we took a break from being productive. Throw out those misconceptions! Rest is good for you and helps you function better when you come back.

First, get enough sleep at night. Go to bed early enough that when you wake naturally you will feel rested. If you have trouble getting to sleep, consider adding some relaxing habits to get ready. Our natural sleep-wake cycle is called a biorhythm for a good reason—it is a rhythmic process that feeds your biological systems. When you're not in the groove, all sorts of things don't work very well.

Find Your Meaning

Live the Stages

Getting Older

Identify Your Goals

Make Helpful Habits

Plan Your Days

Track Your Results

Practice Consistency

Take naps during the day as well. Notice the times of day when you start to feel draggy, and take a nap break to refresh. Most folks feel tired in the early afternoon, but you can develop a sensitivity to your body that will show you when you need a rest. Taking a nap can increase your alertness and productivity, and it's also good for your sense of humor.

Also take time for extended periods of rest and recreation. Just because we're not "working" doesn't mean we don't need vacations. Time away, whether physically or virtually, gives you the chance to step back and see your life from a different angle. I've found that a week or two several times a year can be more effective than a longer time. And of course when you go away, don't make it a high pressure task to see every one of the sights listed in the guidebook.

What goals would help you remember to rest?

Don't Stress Out

We all know that stress can be hazardous to our health, but how can we deal with it? First, realize that some stress is good for us. It keeps us awake and focused. We just need to notice when excitement or anticipation or the desire to do something special has crossed the line and become potentially damaging. We each have warning signs that stress is taking hold—a stiff neck, a churning stomach, a tension headache, a desire to stay in bed all day, etc. What can you do when you feel stressed?

The simplest thing to do in a moment of stress is to use some kind of physical relaxation technique. You can take a moment to consciously clench the muscles of your head, neck and shoulders and then relax them. You can follow your breathing and slow the pace by counting. You can think for a moment of your favorite peaceful place and how it felt the last time you were there.

If you can get away for a few minutes, you can take a break or do a "time out" exercise. Even taking yourself out of the stressful situation can help change your perspective and recharge your batteries. Taking a walk, especially outdoors, can clear your mind and get your blood circulating. A time out, just taking two or three minutes to close your eyes and focus on breathing in and out, can tell your body to relax. Once you're relaxed, you can face the stressful situation with new hope.

When you're dealing with longer-term stress, you need to address the roots of the situation. It can be hard to see the causes of a problem clearly when you're in the middle of it, so stepping outside of it can help. Having someone you can talk to, not to have them fix the problem but just to listen to you explain it, can help. When you describe something, it forces you to distance yourself from it and to see it more objectively. Having someone to talk to often lets you hear the solution that you already knew but couldn't see before.

You can also work on lowering your general vulnerability to stress. Simply experiencing and enjoying calming silence during the day can lower your mind's noise level. Understanding who you are and what you stand for reduces your dependency on the approval of others and the stress it causes. Letting go of guilt for your past failures and mistakes also lowers stress. So does refusing to accept guilt for those things you simply can't do or fix.

What kind of goals would help you reduce and avoid stress?

_____

_____

_____

Manage Your Medical Care

Most of us are used to having bodies that pretty much do what we want them to. We think "walk" and the feet start moving; we think "run" and motion happens. As we age, our bodies have become less responsive and reliable. We can't trade them in on a newer model, so we need to keep them in as good repair as we can.

There has been a great mystique around the wisdom and authority of doctors, but the reality is that doctors are human and medicine is a still-growing body of knowledge. Thinking of doctors and hospitals as the mechanics and repair shops for our body might make things clearer.

You own your body, and you're responsible for the way you care for it. Care for your body includes your physical, emotional, and psychological health. You're the one who knows when things are running well or when, like the squeal in your car's brakes, there's a reason to take it to an expert. If you're puzzled by a symptom, have it investigated.

Of course you need to find experts, doctors and hospitals, that you trust. You also need to find and verify that your sources of information are reliable. Some books, friends, and Internet sites are helpful, and some are not and should be ignored.

Consider your body as like any other appliance you own. Collect and keep your medical records the same way you keep the manuals and repair history of your computer or refrigerator. Keep lists of your medications and dosages over time. When the next thing strikes, you need to know what did and didn't work last time. Know what tests you need regularly and make sure you are having them the same way you make sure the car gets its oil changed.

Make sure that your medical providers can explain things to you in terms you can understand. You need to understand what's going on inside you and what they're doing about it. When someone hands you a pill in the hospital, be sure you know what you're taking and why. Make sure that each person treating you has all the information they need from your other sources, or even carry along your file so they can check it out. Let whoever needs to make a copy, but don't give away originals.

Find Your Meaning

Live the Stages

Getting Older

Identify Your Goals

Make Helpful Habits

Plan Your Days

Track Your Results

Practice Consistency

There are many kinds of tests that you can do at home to monitor your particular conditions. We all know how to take our temperature to check for an infection. Blood pressure monitors are available and easy to use, and they can also tell you your pulse rate. Activity monitors can count your steps and even follow your heart rate while you're exercising. Those of us with diabetes can check our blood sugar with a prick in the morning or during the day. Portable injections for allergic reactions and inhalers for asthma are easy to carry. There are even tiny pills you can take to head off a heart attack.

What kind of goals can you set to get control of your medical care?

_____

_____

_____

All these aspects of your health and fitness are largely under your control. We can't control the aging process, but we can control the way we prepare for it and the way we respond to it.

What goals might you want to establish for your own health and fitness?

_____

_____

_____

_____

_____

_____

_____

_____

_____

How will you recognize success in your health and fitness?

I eat healthy, nutritious small meals # times per day.
I take supplements as needed.
I walk actively every day.
I exercise at least # times a week.
I have a personal trainer and workout # days a week.
I get plenty of sleep.
I take time for extended periods of rest and recreation.
I enjoy doing puzzles and mental exercises every day.
I monitor my stress level and use relaxation techniques to reduce stress.
I am in control of my medical care.

There's happiness in following your vocation and interests and there's happiness in pursuing your personal purpose. These can be very joyful and fulfilling, but they're not the same as smiling, having a great time happiness. And smiling and laughing and having a good time are very good for you.

What kind of things do you just plain like to do? What makes you smile? It's time to make a list. Sometimes just thinking of things to put on the list will make you smile.

_____ _____ _____

_____ _____ _____

_____ _____ _____

_____ _____ _____

_____ _____ _____

_____ _____ _____

_____ _____ _____

_____ _____ _____

Travel

Do consider all the places you'd like to visit – whether short trips or longer adventures. Collect website information, places to stay, activities, locations of interest, local friends and contacts, and medical, visa and insurance details. As you make your plans, think carefully about what you will actually enjoy and make sure to allow time for those activities.

When I was raising young children, I used to look up at the passing airplanes and long to visit the exciting places those people were going. After a few years of traveling for business, I found that they were likely going to see the inside of an airport, an office on the entrance ramp of a highway, and a restaurant where they were too busy thinking about work to enjoy the food.

Now I only travel to see things I want to see and meet people I want to know. I love scenery and local color, but mostly I love the chance to engage with people whose perspective is completely different from mine.

When you think about travel, think of it in terms of what you want to see and do and feel. This isn't a contest to see how many places you've been, but for you to experience the variety of life and lifestyles that the different cultures have to offer.

Find Your Meaning

Live the Stages

Getting Older

Identify Your Goals

Make Helpful Habits

Plan Your Days

Track Your Results

Practice Consistency

Entertainment

We have many, many choices these days, and the entertainment business is constantly inventing more. Even for fun, choose carefully. Don't let a bad film or provocative show ruin your day. Life is too short, and the other choices are too many.

Have a Strategy for Happiness

If you would like to be happier, there are plenty of things you can do to make it happen. Pick some things you can do to build your own strategy:

o Go to everything you possibly can. Buy a ticket to everything you possibly can. Go see everything and experience all you possibly can.

o Think about your particular strengths (ask a friend if you're not sure what they are). Plan ways to use them more in your life.

o Consider nurturing self-esteem, building a supportive network of friends, thinking positively, and being more optimistic.

o For times when things go wrong or you feel down, have a list of small pleasures for cheering yourself up. Build an inventory of mood boosters.

o Develop an "attitude of gratitude" and savor the things you have to be grateful for.

o Since doing things for others makes you feel good as well, explore the opportunities to express more kindness in your life.

Choose to live a vital life. When you live well, it shows in your face and even shows in the sound of your voice.

What goals could you build into your strategy for happiness?

_____

_____

_____

_____

_____

Remove Barriers to Happiness

Get rid of any negative habits of mind that come between you and enjoying your days. For example,

o Lose the negative beliefs you hold about yourself, your life, and your future.

o Challenge your negative beliefs and come up with more empowering ones.

o If you want more optimism, make it a point to notice unhelpful mental habits and choose better ones.

o If you're spending too much time worrying, find a way to tackle the issue or walk away from it.

o Notice grudges you hold against yourself or others, and start to let go.

o Deal with negative habits, like black and white thinking, perfectionism, assuming the worst, catastrophizing, labeling, being a drama queen, taking things personally, deflecting positives, assuming feelings are facts, etc.

What goals could you use to remove your barriers to happiness?

_____

_____

Chipping away at the items that are getting in the way of your happiness will enable you to enjoy the positive more freely.

What goals might you want to set for growing your happiness?

_____

_____

_____

_____

_____

_____

_____

_____

How will you recognize successful progress toward happiness?

I am generally happy and upbeat.
I am confident and optimistic about the future.
I wake up looking forward to having fun.
I rarely worry.
I don't experience any significant negative stress.

Find Your Meaning

Live the Stages

Getting Older

Identify Your Goals

Make Helpful Habits

Plan Your Days

Track Your Results

Practice Consistency

Relationships can be our greatest source of joy or our greatest source of stress, or even both at the same time. Sometimes even a single relationship can be a source of both joy and stress. Even when relationships are a mixed blessing, they're still a blessing because through them we nurture and support each other.

We often take those closest to us for granted, especially those who've been with us for years. If we actually told one person each week that we care about them and how glad we are to have them in our lives, it would keep us conscious of how much each of those around us mean to us.

Family

We retirees tend to live in an all-adult immediate family, sometimes alone and sometimes with a spouse or longtime companion. As we become less able to fend for ourselves, we sometimes have a separate apartment space in the home of one of our adult children.

Grandchildren and acquired grandchildren (nieces and nephews, neighbor children, etc.) are a great joy. The amount of time we can spend with them depends on our own proximity and availability, as well as their stage of childhood. As children get older, their availability and interest in spending time with Gran changes, and we need not to take these changes personally.

> I once asked my grandson whether he would prefer a regular grandma that he saw pretty often or a special events grandma that he saw for holidays and celebrations. He thought a minute and said, "Both." Now that it's painfully clear that I can't throw a football very well, our relationship has changed somewhat. He teaches me.

Our relationships with adult children are probably the most important and sensitive we have. They've made the transition from dependent to independent, and as we go on our roles will be reversed. As my son once said, "You should be nice to me because I'm the one who's going to choose your nursing home." We're going to need increasing amounts of help and support as we age, and we need to have good relationships with younger adults that we trust.

It's critically important that we prepare in advance for the time when we will not be able to make decisions for ourselves, particularly in the area of medical care. When there's a sudden illness or accident, there will be decisions to make about care and treatment, and we will not be in a position to make them.

Whether it's a grown child, a friend, or a professional like a lawyer or trustee, we need to have someone in place to defend our interests. That person should not only have our instructions for situations we can anticipate, but also know us well enough to figure out what we'd want to do in a situation we didn't think about.

We need to know someone that we can trust with our life and our future, and we need to talk with that person so they understand what we think and hope for. This is a difficult conversation, but it's better to have it when both are relaxed and able to think clearly, rather than in a hospital emergency room.

What areas in your relationships with your family need attention?

_____

_____

_____

_____

_____

Friends

Friendship is probably the greatest support system in the world. Close friends are those wonderful people who know all about you and still like you. Casual friends are those with whom you have something in common, perhaps a shared interest or some common experiences. We all need some of both kinds.

There's typically only enough time to keep regular contact with three to five close friends, if we are lucky enough to find so many. With close friends, you know what's going on in their lives, and they know what's going on in yours. It takes regular interaction and time to communicate in depth. Texting or tweeting won't do it. You need to spend time together at least every week or so, to stay connected.

A close friend is someone you can call in a crisis, someone who will come and rescue you from a mess or help hold you together when you're coming apart. And when you get that kind of a call from a close friend, you put down what you were doing and reach for the car keys. A close friend is someone who, when they need to talk, you will make time to listen. And vice versa.

At this age, there may be people out there in the world who have been close friends at other stages of life. This is a good time to reach out to those we've known, to let them know that we still care about them and remember them, and also to undo any misunderstanding or bad feelings that may have been left over. We can also enjoy just talking over the past together, sharing memories and sharing the places we've been while we were apart.

What might you want to do to strengthen current friendships and revisit old ones?

_____

_____

_____

_____

Find Your Meaning

Live the Stages

Getting Older

Identify Your Goals

Make Helpful Habits

Plan Your Days

Track Your Results

Practice Consistency

What goals might help you develop and improve your relationships?

_____

_____

_____

_____

_____

_____

_____

_____

How will you recognize success in your relationships?

My relationships are one of my greatest sources of joy.
I have a best friend who accepts me for who I am.
I have a best friend with whom I can share my dreams and my fears.
I have a group of close friends that I see regularly.
I have younger close friends or relatives I can trust with my welfare.
I enjoy being with my friends and feel refreshed and energized when we are together.

Environment

Your personal environment is the place you live. It may be the house or apartment you've lived in for years, or it may be new, chosen to fit the changes in your activities and needs. If we choose to stay in the same place, we know that we'll need to make some changes to adapt it to our new limitations.

As we have less energy and time to spend, it's important to find substitutes for some of our tasks of daily living, like housework, food preparation, laundry, and repairs.

As we're less able to do some of the things we used to do easily, it's important to find alternative ways to cope. This is particularly important when it comes to our ability to get around. Just when we need to be proactive to get to doctors' appointments and gatherings with friends, our ability to walk or drive can deteriorate.

Anticipating and planning changes to our environment and support systems allows us to create the situation we want to live in, rather than being forced by circumstances into whatever is available at the time we need it.

Home

There's an old saying that anything that goes wrong with a house can be fixed with two books: a phonebook and a checkbook. This is almost true except for two factors: one must use the books and there needs to be unlimited money in the checking account.

Since lots of things can go wrong with a house (failing hot water heaters, falling trees, backing up sewage, and many more), the energy to find fixers and the money to pay them are at risk of depletion. Finding an appropriate place to live or keeping the current one functioning take work and planning.

Living comfortably in your place, wherever that place turns out to be, also takes work and planning. The principle that physics calls "entropy" says that left alone, things just naturally get messy. Keeping your living space from being overwhelmed by clutter takes organization, constant maintenance, and life simplification.

Simplification includes looking at the possessions you've accumulated over the years and figuring out their future. Some things you just love, either for themselves or for their memories. You might enjoy passing some of them on with their stories. There are lots of other things, though, that you might consider finding other homes for, either as donations, consignments, or to the swap table.

How could you make your current living situation more livable? How can you set up your living space so that it will take less time and energy to maintain?

Find Your Meaning

Live the Stages

Getting Older

Identify Your Goals

Make Helpful Habits

Plan Your Days

Track Your Results

Practice Consistency

What specific goals can you put in place to move in the right direction?

_____

_____

_____

Finances

There are a lot of books about how to plan for retirement financially, but for most of us that window has closed. There are also lots of books and advisors that would like to help us with our money, of course while keeping a piece of it for themselves. It's important to find advice and advisors you can trust.

Getting more informed is always good, though. I recommend the local adult classes on retirement planning, because they give you a chance to hear what a professional has to say before you become a client. The reality of the financial markets is that no one has a crystal ball, and no one can predict what will happen next. Even basing decisions on past experience is like driving while looking in the rear view mirror.

You may want to plan to get help with ordinary financial affairs like paying bills and dealing with taxes. It's also good as well to have one or more trusted members of the younger generation aware of your financial situation and where to find critical papers, like wills, health care proxies, and power of attorney.

What goals might you set to keep control of your finances?

_____

_____

_____

Transportation

Mobility is critical in our current culture, and we all want to stay mobile as long as possible. There will come a time when, either by our own choice or at the urging of others, we will have to give up our independent driving. This can be a very painful decision, since freedom of the road is a pervasive value in our culture. The time to face this loss will come to most of us, and it helps to know how we will handle it when the time comes.

The availability of transportation services is dependent on where you live.
o Services like "the Ride" in the Boston area make it possible for disabled folks to get to doctors, church, and meetings independently.
o Taxis and ride share services are readily available in some places but not others.
o Senior living complexes often have vans for group and individual travel.
o Some churches arrange to match parishioners with those who need rides.
o Some retired businessmen have been known to hire retired veterans as drivers.
o Some teens have been known to provide transportation in exchange for the money to pay their auto insurance.
Creativity is the key to finding alternatives to having a car and driving yourself.

Is there a goal that you can make to plan for your transportation needs?

_____

_____

_____

What goals might you want to set that improve your overall living environment?

_____

_____

_____

_____

_____

How will you recognize success in your environment?

The clutter isn't taking over my world.
I can find things I'm looking for.
I know how to get things fixed when they are broken.
My finances and spending are under control.
The bills and taxes are paid regularly.
I can get around safely, and I have a plan for times I don't feel comfortable driving.

Find Your Meaning

Live the Stages

Getting Older

Identify Your Goals

Make Helpful Habits

Plan Your Days

Track Your Results

Practice Consistency

Living Your Spirituality

Some of us think of ourselves as spiritual but not religious. Others of us are committed to one of the world's religious traditions. Still others are exploring the possibilities. There are even some who want nothing to do with spirituality at all. As a Christian and a Presbyterian minister I have my convictions, but I think that each of us must make our own choice.

Each of the world's religions has an understanding of what will happen to us after death. Many of the practices of the religions are aimed at preparing people for that end. Buddhists learn to meditate and leave desires behind because this will prepare them for the endless peace of Nirvana. Christians are supposed to learn to love neighbors and even enemies, since we'll spend a lot of time in each other's company in heaven.

The world's religions agree at many points on what is good and how we should live. Almost all agree that human beings are a work-in-progress that still needs improvement.

Whatever your spirituality, it probably includes some recommendations for self-improvement. It probably also includes some instructions about work you should be doing while you are in the world.

What goals can you put in place to do what your faith asks of you?

_____

_____

_____

_____

Spirituality Near the End of Life

Studies have shown that people who have a faith tend to be healthier and live longer than those who don't. The problem is that it is not enough to go through the motions; you have to actually believe. Knowing and really believing that you know where you're going helps you get there.

If you know what the end will hold for you, you can figure out what preparations you need to make for it. If you're not sure, this is a good time to be asking questions and listening to the answers. In either case, this is a really good time to enjoy and savor every moment we have on the green side of the grass.

What goals might you choose to deepen and strengthen your faith? What kinds of spirituality would you like to explore?

_____

_____

_____

Jerry's Dad

Jerry told me about his experience with his father near the end of his father's life. Jerry is not a person of faith, but his dad was a lifelong believing Christian. Jerry was taking his father from the hospital to spend his last few days at home. To his surprise, Jerry found that his father was actually happy, looking forward to the end with eager anticipation. "Now I'm finally going to find out if it's all true!" he said. He couldn't wait to find out how all of the promises of a lifetime of faith would finally turn out.

What goals might you want to set that improve your spiritual life?

_____

_____

_____

_____

_____

_____

How will you recognize success in care for your spiritual life?

I feel connected to God.
I actively pursue spiritual development.
I feel my life has meaning and purpose.
I am an active participant in my faith community.
I am constantly aware of God's presence in my life.
I am consistent in my spiritual disciplines.
I am clear about my purpose and how it relates to God's larger story.

Find Your Meaning

Live the Stages

Getting Older

Identify Your Goals

Make Helpful Habits

Plan Your Days

Track Your Results

Practice Consistency

Choose Your Current Goals

As you consider what goals you'd like to have for the next few weeks or months, go back over your thoughts about each of the areas of life. To start, you might choose the one most important goal that came out of your consideration in each area. You may want to add one or two more, if there's more than one item in an area that is high priority.

As you look at each potential goal, consider:
o What's my target deadline? When do I want to achieve this goal?
o What are the activities I need to do to get me to my goal?
o What activities can I do every day that will move me toward my goal?
o How will I measure my activities?
o How often will I measure those activities?
o How can I keep myself accountable?
o Are there rewards I can give myself along the way?

Don't forget that the activities to get to the goal need to be things that are under your control. Winning the lottery isn't under your control, but putting in time on a task is.

Make a preliminary list of the goals you'd like to achieve. You may want to live with the list for a few days, thinking about your goals and how you will feel when they've been accomplished. You may also want to think about the way the activities needed for the different goals work together or complement each other.

Selecting goals is not a once-for-all process. The goal setting process is fluid over time, and you'll have plenty of opportunities to fine tune or even change directions. Your first set of goals is not set in concrete, so pick some that feel right and make a start.

Your current set of goals will evolve and change as time goes on. Some goals you will accomplish. Some goals you will decide that you didn't really want after all. For some goals, you'll find that you still want to get there, but that you need to find a better way or new or different activities to get there. You'll have a chance to look at and think about how your goals are working each week when you plan for your coming week.

When you pursue goals, often life does not cooperate. When insurmountable obstacles get in the way, that's the time to regroup. This requires that you change your goals in order to get around the obstacle that's in your way. When you're pursuing any dream you will have to make changes from time to time. It's just part of the process, so there's no need to feel discouraged about it.

Capture Each Goal in Detail

When you have your preliminary list of goals, it's time to think them through in detail. Make a copy of the goal worksheet for each goal you're planning, and maybe some spares to use as you go along.

First you need to write the goal very clearly and specifically. Writing down why it's important and why it matters to you will show you why the goal is worth the time and effort to do. In times of discouragement, this will remind you of why you wanted to follow this goal in the first place.

Then you need to think about the end point for the goal. How, exactly, will you know that you got there? It's important that each goal have some kind of fixed end point. Otherwise you can't get there and might as well be on a hamster wheel. Once you know what success will look and feel like, you need to anticipate when that will happen. Making this time specific will anchor your hoped for success in the real world.

Next you need to consider what achieving the goal will take. Are the steps to be taken under your control and doable? Where will you get the resources you need, whether they are time, money, expertise, skills, or whatever? Who will help you, and who will you depend on for ongoing support or participation?

Then there is a really important question, how will you be accountable? Since these are personal goals, you won't have a boss checking to see if you're making progress. You need to be your own boss, and keep track of your own progress. You also need to recruit a friend or associate to help you stay focused. It can be a little as a weekly conversation or phone call, but you need someone who will ask you how it's going and really listen to the answer.

The next step is to think about the obstacles you're likely to encounter and how you'll overcome them. This is of course not fun, since you don't want negative thinking to dampen your enthusiasm. But the reality is that if you don't think ahead, discovering the obstacles will be a bad surprise that could throw you off track. Knowing in advance what you will do when an obstacle comes up gives you the confidence that you know what you need to do when the time comes.

Finally, you come to the meat of the work, the actual activities that you will do to make the goal a reality. You need to break the work up into small, manageable activities that you can plan, do, and finish. I like to use activities that can fit into half of a day, a couple of two hour chunks. Of course some activities can be done more quickly and others will need to be split into several parts as you discover how much time they actually take. You can always make changes as you go along, but to start you need to make as accurate estimates as you can. Your plan will then show your steps to get to your goal.

Find Your Meaning

Live the Stages

Getting Older

Identify Your Goals

Make Helpful Habits

Plan Your Days

Track Your Results

Practice Consistency

Goal Worksheet Sample

Goal: *make retirement control workbook*   **Life Area:** *vocation*

What will you accomplish?	*create a workbook for organizing time and energy in retirement and circulate it to retirees*
Why is this important?	*there is a lot written about financial stuff, but not much to do with how to decide what to do next*
Why does it matter to you?	*I need to get organized too*
How will you know it's done?	*when it is available and people are using it*
When will it be done?	*written, reviewed, and edited by fall, out by Christmas*
Is it realistic? Can it be done?	*probably, if folks relate to it and if I stay functional*
Where will you get resources?	*friends and colleagues for reviewers, hopefully an agent for placement*
Who will you get involved?	*everybody I talk to who is retired or knows someone who is*

How will you be accountable for progress?

weekly progress reports to core group (husband, accountability partner, therapist)

What obstacles can you expect?	How will you handle them?
I am lousy at marketing	*try to find some professional (agent) who could make money on it*
I need to minimize stress	*try not to take interest in the workbook (or lack of it) personally*

Action Steps	Date	Done?
1 *finish text of chapter 8*		
2 *build examples for sample to-do, week, goal & habit tracking*		
3 *format manuscript with tabs on pages*		
4 *print copies for retiree group*		
5 *create feedback form for reviewers*		
6 *present initial version to retiree group*	*May 4*	
7 *write proposal and letter to send to possible agents*		
8 *incorporate group feedback into manuscript*		
9 *print copies for reviewers*		
10 *circulate copies to reviewers*		
11 *incorporate reviewer feedback*		
12 *print and mail proposal and copies to agents*		

Goal Worksheet

Goal: _____ **Life Area:** _____

What will you accomplish?	
Why is this important?	
Why does it matter to you?	
How will you know it's done?	
When will it be done?	
Is it realistic? Can it be done?	
Where will you get resources?	
Who will you get involved?	

How will you be accountable for progress?

_____

_____

What obstacles can you expect?	How will you handle them?

Action Steps	Done?	Date
1		
2		
3		
4		
5		
6		
7		
8		
9		
10		
11		
12		
13		
14		

Goal: _____ **Life Area:** _____

Action Steps	Done?	Date
15		
16		
17		
18		
19		
20		
21		
22		
23		
24		
25		
26		
27		
28		
29		
30		
31		
32		
33		
34		
35		
36		
37		
38		
39		
40		
41		
42		
43		
44		
45		
46		
47		
48		
49		
50		
51		
52		
53		
54		

5. Make Helpful Habits

Find Your Meaning

Live the Stages

Getting Older

Identify Your Goals

Make Helpful Habits

Plan Your Days

Track Your Results

Practice Consistency

As a child of the 60's, I used to think that habits or any kind of routine behavior were boring and uncreative. More recently I've discovered that habits make it possible to deal with uninteresting tasks without a lot of effort.

Habits Save Time and Energy

There are just so many things we can pay attention to at one time or in one day. That number gets smaller as we get older. How can we make room in our time and attention for all the things we need and want to do?

One way to save the time for making decisions is not to have to make a decision each time we do something. If we already know what comes next or always do the same thing because it's Tuesday, we don't have to make a decision about it every time.

Picture this by thinking about taking a shower. You can always start at the top and move down, or you can do the pieces in whatever order feels good at the time. If I first feel like washing my face, then the feet, then shampoo, I have to remember whether or not I did the elbows yet. Doing things in the same order makes it easier to be sure that the whole job gets done.

It's Tuesday

Weekly patterns also simplify thinking about what happens next. Having days for particular activities leads to very predictable patterns (banking on Mondays, groceries on Tuesdays, bridge on Fridays, etc.). You only have to remember what day of the week it is and you're set.

Patterns save time and energy in deciding what to do when. They allow collecting related ideas and tasks into batches, and they provide a sense of security through familiar experiences and predictability.

You Just Have to Show Up

The simplest way to keep on track is to have all you need for an activity ready and in place when it's time to do it. Then you only have to show up, and the activity will happen automatically. When you have the things you need and your plans for what to do next all ready to use, right where you'll see them, you can just get going. There's no need to think about it or make decisions.

Once you know what your goals are and roughly what things you'll have to do to accomplish them, it's time to build some habits that will help get you there. Some of the activities for a goal will need to be done in order because they build on each other, and some will need to be done over and over.

You need to create two kinds of habits, one kind to insure that you have time set aside to do the activities that build on each other, and the other kind to make sure that you do the activities that need to be repeated every day. We want the work toward our goals to become effortless and automatic, so we don't have to use

49

willpower and discipline to get things done. We need to build the progress toward our goals into our days, every day.

Analyze Your Usual Schedule

First you need to be sure you have a complete list of the things you want to fit into your day. You start by figuring out where you're currently spending your time.

The most effective way is to keep a record of what you are doing every half hour for a couple of weeks. There's an activity log form at the end of this section if you're willing or able to do a complete log. You keep the log form with you during the day and write down what you find yourself doing each half hour.

Another way is to guess roughly how much time you're spending each day, week, and month on the activities you do regularly. Below is a sample of the kinds of things you might include. An empty current activity worksheet for this approach is also at the end of this section.

activity	length	frequency	when it happens
daily			
breakfast	¼ hr	1/day	8~9
local walk	½ hr	1/day	
nap	2 hr	1/day	1-3 or 4-6
weekly			
groceries	2-3 hr	1/wk	
grandkids	5 hr	1/wk	Wednesday
church	4 hr	1/wk	Sunday am
monthly			
support group		1/mth	1st Tuesday
committee meeting		1/mth	
as needed			
doctor			
physical therapists			

Look at the activities you are currently doing either from the log or from the worksheet, and think about where they fit into one of three groups:
- things that are important that you want to get done
- basic stuff you need and want to do regularly
- fluff that doesn't have a particular value to you

Things that are important to you should probably be part of your overall goals. Check back over your existing goals to see if these are activities that should be included in your current goals. If not, you may want to think about why you're doing them and perhaps create a new goal around the reasons they are important to you.

Basic things you need and want to continue to do regularly should be made into automatic habits.

What Automatic Habits Do You Need?

Those activities that need to be done over and over, like exercise or medications, need to be built into every day. First thing in the morning and last thing before bed are good times to build in these habits, but you can also create times for them during the day as well.

The first step to ensuring a good day is a little planning the night before. If you take about ten minutes to think about the day ahead, you'll wake up knowing what comes next, with a vision of the day to come. In the evening, you should:
o   remember (and note) the successes of the day you just finished
o   identify the most important things you need to do tomorrow
o   decide (and put out) what you'll wear

Begin each day with habits that will get you mind and body started in the right direction. To get each day off to a good start, don't forget to:
o   eat a good breakfast
o   exercise to get your body working
o   touch base with your purpose and your motivation
o   visualize the things you'll be doing
o   plan to do one nasty task first to get it out of the way
Getting one unpleasant task taken care of early in the day will take a weight off your mind and make all the other activities you plan feel much easier. Getting one task done that you've been avoiding also gives you a burst of satisfaction and positive energy.

As the day goes on, you may want to add times for other regular habits that you want to happen automatically. You might consider:
o   a nap
o   a drink and a snack
o   a walk outdoors
o   silence or meditation
o   whatever refreshes and re-energizes you
Only you will know how to put in these habits for refreshment when you find yourself at a low point.

Winding down at the end of the day should leave you relaxed and ready for a good night's restful sleep. Only you know what you will find relaxing. You may have some regular choices, but exploring new possibilities can widen your options. I find mindless puzzles relaxing, but I know folks who get more tense about getting the right answer. Some like jazz or classical music, but I like just plain quiet. You need to know what works for you. The day then closes when you:
o   make your plans for tomorrow and let go of them
o   use a relaxation process (music, puzzles, undemanding TV, light reading)
o   prepare for bed and sleep

Make a List of Your Desired Habits

Look through your goals to see what activities you should put into these habit periods during the day. Typically health and fitness goals include activities that

Find Your Meaning

Live the Stages

Getting Older

Identify Your Goals

Make Helpful Habits

Plan Your Days

Track Your Results

Practice Consistency

happen regularly, and the one way to make sure they happen is to make them automatic.

You may also want to list any other regular activities that are important to you. This could include journaling or keeping a diary, spiritual readings or scripture, prayer or meditation, social media or traditional correspondence, telephone time or even simply personal quiet time.

Look at your desirable habit list and make sure that they really are things that you want to do often and regularly. Habits are meant to build things you want to do into your life. They're not a time to try to sneak in things you really hate to do but think you "should" be doing. Don't sabotage your helpful habits by building in an obstacle that could derail them.

Plan Your Daily Routine

Build the daily habits you want to become automatic into a daily structure. The daily habit worksheet can help you organize the habits you'd like to establish.

These habits will go into a check-off list that will be part of your plan for each week, as you'll see in the next chapter. At first, having the list will be a reminder of what to do next, so you won't have to think about it. As you go forward, the check marks will help you see which habits are working and which aren't. You'll be able to make changes in your routine, to change the order of the habits or even change their times of day, to make them more comfortable for you in the long term.

Eventually the habits will become automatic, and you may not need to use the checks. Returning to using the checks will help you get back into the routine when you've been away for a while. It will also help, when you make a change in routine, to remind you of the new pattern while it's being established.

The worksheet has a list of some sample habits, but you should also add your own, some from your current activities, some from the goal activities you want to do every day, and to make regular space for other goal activities. Check or circle the habits on the suggestion list that you'd like to make, and put any other habits you'd like to have on the lines below the suggestion list.

Think about how you would group your habits, first by time of day, and then by how they flow from one habit to the next. Then fill in the habits you'd like to start with in the column on the right, grouped into morning, mid-day, and evening habits. Include all the items you really want to become regular.

Day by Day Activity Log
Note the primary activity in each time period.

time	Sun	Mon	Tues	Wed	Thurs	Fri	Sat
6-6:30							
6:30-7							
7-7:30							
7:30-8							
8-8:30							
8:30-9							
9-9:30							
9:30-10							
10-10:30							
10:30-11							
11-11:30							
11:30-12							
12-12:30							
12:30-1							
1-1:30							
1:30-2							
2-2:30							
2:30-3							
3-3:30							
3:30-4							
4-4:30							
4:30-5							
5-5:30							
5:30-6							
6-6:30							
6:30-7							
7-7:30							
7:30-8							
8-8:30							
8:30-9							
9-9:30							
9:30-10							
10-10:30							
10:30-11							
11-11:30							
11:30-12							

Find Your Meaning

Live the Stages

Getting Older

Identify Your Goals

Make Helpful Habits

Plan Your Days

Track Your Results

Practice Consistency

Current Activities Worksheet

activity	length	frequency	when it happens
daily			
weekly			
monthly			
as needed			

Daily Habit Worksheet

Identify the habits you want to create and place them in time periods.

morning grooming (teeth, hair, etc.)
exercise / physical therapy
coffee
bath or shower
dress
breakfast
consider your purpose
review goals and direction
finalize plan for the day
plan one obnoxious task first
email / social media

local walk
workout / cardio / strength training
rest / nap

review day's successes
make tomorrow's plans
final email / social media
unwind (read, TV, puzzles, ...)
bath or shower
undress for bed
relaxation: tea / medication
music
sleep

morning

during the day

evening

Find Your Meaning

Live the Stages

Getting Older

Identify Your Goals

Make Helpful Habits

Plan Your Days

Track Your Results

Practice Consistency

6. Plan Your Days and Week

Using our time the way we want to use it actually takes planning. We want to keep in mind the things that are important to us as we go along. It's too easy to come to the end of an activity and go on to whatever seems easiest or comes to mind at the time. Planning helps our reality match our intentions.

Organize Your Ordinary Day

First, think about the things you'd like to have happen in an ordinary day. You're retired, remember, and you are your own boss. At first we may be reacting to the freedom from our old jobs and just want to lie in bed all day. But once we start to think about living forward, we have choices, not only about what we want to do, but also about when and how we'll do it.

Write down in broad terms what a perfect day would look like for you. If you could have anything you wanted, the people you want to spend your time with, the time you'd be spending doing different things, what would that be? Design your perfect day.

How does your day work? Are you a morning person or a night person? When do you do your best thinking, and when do you have the most energy? When do you usually need rest? What happens when you get over tired? What pattern of meals works for you? You might want to live with your perfect day for a little while, because ideas about what you want to include could come to you at any time.

Once you're clear about the things you want to have in your day, create a flow for it. Build in times for meals and snacks, rest, activities, and habits. Picture yourself getting up in the morning with this day ahead of you. How would you feel? How would you fine-tune it?

Make a Habit of Daily Progress

One of the things you want to be sure to build into your perfect day is progress toward the goals that matter to you. Sometimes it's a shock to discover that our actual use of time doesn't match our priorities. Once we notice the mismatch, we can deal with the areas we need to bring into alignment.

At the end of each day, note the activities you have completed. Give yourself a star in the **Done** column for every activity completed. At the end of the week you'll have a nice collection of stars to show what you've accomplished.

One way to picture our time available is as a glass where we want to put some rocks, gravel, sand, and water. If we put the sand in first, there's no room for the rocks. Activities toward goals are the rocks that we want to be sure have time. After them we can add the gravel, habits we need every day. Then we can add the sand, less critical activities that fit in around the others. Last we can add the water, low value activities that we want to keep.

Find Your Meaning

Live the Stages

Getting Older

Identify Your Goals

Make Helpful Habits

Plan Your Days

Track Your Results

Practice Consistency

Does your perfect day reflect your goal priorities? Take time to think about and arrange your goals in order of importance. The idea is to be clear about what really matters to you in order to make sure you're using your time well.

Now look at your idea of the perfect day. How can you arrange it so that your time used matches your priorities? Make sure that your time is put first to your highest priority goals and that this time is protected from wasting. Then include places for the other habits you want to cultivate.

As we create the plan for each day, we need to build in the time for progress on our goals. For many of us, this will be easiest if we set aside the same time every day for a particular goal. For others, creating several working periods where we simply move on to the next activity on the list will work as well. The key is that every day we come to a point where we know and expect that the next thing we will do is work toward one of our goals. And if the activity is there ready to do, we only have to show up and start.

If you decide your priorities when you plan your week, then the habit of working on your current goal next can take over. The key is to expect that you will always be doing something toward a goal when the time comes. Then when that time comes, you look at the week's plan to know exactly what the current activity will be.

Part of the progress habit is that, at the end of your time on any activity, you clean up the things you used for it and get out the things you'll need for the next one. What you'll be doing next is freshest when you've just been engaged and busy, so this is the very best time to set up for the next patch of progress.

Guard against Losing Time

While we're looking at things we want to build into our days, we should also look at things we want to not take up time during our days. These are the things we're used to doing that eat up our productive time without providing any value.

Some things just take up all available time. For those of us who were housewives before women's lib, we know that housework can take up all day, every day. Now our time is too valuable to let disappear into a black hole. Current activities that can expand to use all available time include social media, surfing the Internet, computer games, and even forms of Solitaire. Now we need to limit the amount of time they can take. Social media, for example, can be restricted to one or two periods per day, with a timer set if necessary.

Do you have a habit of doing something you don't really enjoy? Look at your relaxation time to see that what you're doing really is leaving you relaxed and refreshed. If it isn't providing value, stop it and recover the wasted time.

We can also be stuck in behaviors that absorb precious time. Procrastination is one of the all-time biggest eaters of time. Second guessing and agonizing over decisions is another one. Letting others take advantage of our time and attention is yet another. Trying to do too many things at once, none of them well, wastes time and takes time to correct our mistakes. Don't let any of these time drains find regular space in your day.

It's also good to check for distractions that waste your time. Are interruptions keeping you from getting things done? Take a look at your interruptions and distractions. Is the sound from the radio, TV, or someone else's entertainment pulling your attention away? Are interruptions and demands coming from other people destroying your focus? Consider turning off the phone, silencing notifications, or making yourself "unavailable" for the time you need to concentrate.

Take a hard look at your existing commitments. Are they providing the value they used to or that you expected when you made them? Consider reducing some of the non-essential commitments. If you reduce at least a few commitments, you'll now have room in your life for more of the things you want to do — including your personal goals.

Do you have any activities that feel virtuous but actually waste time? Paper shuffling? Meetings? Over-planning/organizing? Excessive email checking? Make them go away!

Finally, do you have people in your life who consistently leave you drained and exhausted? Instead of suffering in silence or getting mad, for each energy-drain in your life, consider:
o What exactly drains me
o Whether it's short or long-term (i.e., whether it will sort itself out in time)
o How I could act differently
o What I could say
o How I could reduce the time I spend with that person.

Choose Your Week's Activities

This is where we actually make our to-do list. We begin with our current goal sheets. Look down the list of activities to see the progress you have made so far. Then consider which of the next activities would fit into the coming week and move them onto the To-Do list for that goal. Make sure that some of the most important as well as most urgent activities are included.

Use the first column of the To-Do list for the goals and put the activities in the second column. If any of the activities have hard deadlines (or you want to be firm about them), note the dates in the Due Date column.

This is the time to balance and blend the different kinds of activities you want in your week. Don't let any important area be short-changed, whether it's friendship, work on the house, or just plain fun. Plan to keep the To-Do list where you will see it often during the day and week.

Build in Your Habits

Now it's time to build the habits you want to establish into each day of your week. Go back to your Daily Habit Worksheet and move the morning, evening, and mid-

Find Your Meaning

Live the Stages

Getting Older

Identify Your Goals

Make Helpful Habits

Plan Your Days

Track Your Results

Practice Consistency

day habits into the first column of the habit list. Keeping the list where you'll see it often, especially at the morning, evening, and mid-day times when you want to reinforce the habits, will remind you of what comes next.

The columns on the habit list are for checking off each habit as you do it. Yes, this does seem compulsive, but it will help fix the routine in your mind. After a few weeks of doing the same habits in the same order, the move from one to the next won't take much thought.

What Do You Want to Keep in Mind?

Below the habits on the To-Do list form are some questions and statements of intention. These are to help you keep in mind specific thoughts and attitudes that you want to focus on during the week.

Keeping these in front of you with your habit and To-Do activity lists will remind you to think about them.

This is the place to note a person you are concerned about or a problem that you need to think through. It is also a place to remind yourself of something you want to make happen—a way you want to feel, a blessing you want to be thankful for, or even an attitude you want to leave behind. It is a place to remind yourself of the kind of person you want to grow into as well as the kind of people and experiences you want to attract.

This is a place for reminders of helpful or healing thoughts that you want to come back to. You can use it to establish and reinforce ways of thinking that ground you and give you hope.

Make Your Week's Schedule

At the beginning of the week, either Sunday evening or Monday morning, it's time to organize your habits and activities for the week. First, of course, you need to fill in the commitments that have a fixed day and time, like meetings and appointments, on the Weekly Activity Plan. But what next?

I like to picture each day as having five two-hour activity periods, two in the morning, two in the afternoon, and one in the early evening. I also like to make activities small enough that they can fit into two hours, although sometimes an activity may need twice that.

As a morning person, I like to have the most demanding activities early in the day. Not only does this mean that I am fresher, but planning the night before allows whatever creative ideas I might have to percolate overnight.

I like to have a break or a treat in the afternoon, so an errand with a friend or play time with a grandchild fits in nicely. For me, evening is a good time for detail work, organizing or bringing things together. Times when I am tired or winding down are good for editing or Internet research.

Each of us has our own productivity pattern, and only you know what works best for you. As you place your planned activities on the Weekly Activity Plan calendar, be sure to balance them across the week as well as within each day.

Above all, don't forget to put your highest priority activities into prime time, whatever that time is for you. When you're done with the week's calendar, step back and look at the week as a whole to make any adjustments that will help it flow smoothly.

Live One Day at a Time

Once your plans for the week are in place you won't have to worry or think about them, except for a brief review in the morning and evening. In each moment of the day, you can be completely engaged in what you're doing without being distracted by thoughts about the past or future.

As you go through the week, you'll find that most days don't work out exactly as planned. Some activities take longer than you expected. Some need to be broken up into smaller pieces. Some don't actually need to happen at all. Some that you hadn't thought of suddenly appear.

Each evening when you anticipate the next day, make whatever changes you need in the week's plan. The plan isn't a taskmaster you have to satisfy but an assistant to help you stay on track. It can only help you if you're flexible and adjust it to match the reality of what you want to be and do.

Find Your Meaning

Live the Stages

Getting Older

Identify Your Goals

Make Helpful Habits

Plan Your Days

Track Your Results

Practice Consistency

Sample To-Do List

Goal	Activity	Due	Done
writing	finish text of chapter 8		
	make sample to-do, week, tracking		
	format/check manuscript & tabs		
	print & bind copies for group		
	present to group	5 / 4	
	collect feedback		
	plan sermon for Pentecost		
knitting	find pattern for vest		
medical	get dentist appointment		
	go to dentist		
fun	day trip to NH antiquing		
	sailboat cleaning		
family	grandson Will overnight		
	dinner with daughter Mary		
friends	lunch with Val		
	shopping with Kitty		
	visit with Tim		
	prayer group		
home	yard work		
	set up new printer		
faith	women's retreat at church		
	Sunday worship		

Week of _____

Habits	M	T	W	T	F	S	S
morning							
getting up routine							
exercise / physical therapy							
bath or shower							
dress							
breakfast							
consider purpose question							
review goals and direction							
day plan w/intentions							
set one unpleasant task first							
email / social media							
short local walk							
during the day							
exercise							
rest							
evening							
review goals and intentions							
tomorrow's plan list							
final email							
unwind (tv, knitting, …)							
bath or shower							
undress for bed							
relax: tea / medication							
light reading / puzzles							
sleep							

What is most important? Who is most important?

I want to be	
I want to feel	
I want to appreciate	
I want to let go of	
I want to attract	

Sample Weekly Activity Plan

Period	Monday	Tuesday	Wednesday	Thursday	Friday	Saturday	Sunday
8:00 breakfast							
1: 9:00	boat work	make workbook copies	bind copies to hand out	day trip to NH antiques	plan sermon for next week	day retreat at church	church
10:00							
2: 11:00			retiree grp mtg presentation		lunch with Val		
12:00		prayer group					
1:00 lunch	lunch with Mary						take Will home
3: 2:00			make notes to incorporate feedback		visit deck place with Kitty		grocery shop
3:00	nap	nap	rest	visit with Tim		nap	
4: 4:00	finish text of chapter 8						
5:00		set up new printer				Will overnight	
6:00 supper							
5: 7:00	format/check manuscript						
8:00							
9:00							
sleep							
What worked or didn't?							

Find Your Meaning | Live the Stages | Getting Older | Identify Your Goals | Make Helpful Habits | **Plan Your Days** | Track Your Results | Practice Consistency

To-Do List

Goal	Activity	Due	Done
vocation			
interests			
health			
happiness			
family			
relationships			
environment			
spirituality			

Week of _____

Habits	M	T	W	T	F	S	S
morning							
review goals and direction							
make day plan (w/intentions)							
plan one obnoxious task first							
during the day							
exercise							
rest							
evening							
review goals and intentions							
tomorrow's plan list							
unwind							
relaxation							
sleep							
review goals and intentions							
tomorrow's plan list							

What is most important? Who is most important?

I want to be	
I want to feel	
I want to appreciate	
I want to let go of	
I want to attract	

Weekly Activity Plan

Period	Monday	Tuesday	Wednesday	Thursday	Friday	Saturday	Sunday
8:00 breakfast							
1: 9:00							
10:00							
2: 11:00							
12:00							
1:00 lunch							
3: 2:00							
3:00							
4: 4:00							
5:00							
6:00 supper							
5: 7:00							
8:00							
9:00							
sleep							
What worked or didn't?							

Find Your Meaning	Live the Stages	Getting Older	Identify Your Goals	Make Helpful Habits	Plan Your Days	Track Your Results	Practice Consistency

7. Track Your Results

The problem with most to-do lists is that when you finish a task you cross it off the list. Crossing things off is the only time you get a sense of satisfaction. Some folks put things they already did on the list, just to have the fun of crossing them off. All you have in front of you most of the time is the mass of things you still have to do. You can only see the work ahead and not the overall progress so far.

Why Take the Time to Track?

Taking the time to track what you've accomplished lets you see how far you've come. It lets you see your achievements and feel a sense of accomplishment. It establishes momentum in the direction of your goals. It gives you a chance to appreciate your own work on one side and to feel that someone has noticed what you are doing on the other.

Research has shown that accountability, especially through weekly progress reporting, is critical to successfully achieving goals. In addition, public commitment to goals and public acknowledgment of progress are important contributors to ultimate success. This is the secret of the effectiveness of support groups for those making changes, like AA and Weight Watchers.

Since accountability is the key to being able to stick with resolutions, tracking is the basis for recognizing our progress. We need to be able to measure our progress, and recording what we got done every day gives us the information we need. The most effective form of accountability includes not only recording progress, but also reporting it and making it public.

See Progress toward Your Goals

Every time you transition from one week to the next, it's time to move from one group of planned activities to the next. This is when you look back over the week that was to see what you've accomplished.

As you look back over your To-Do list, you'll find that a number of goal activities have been marked done. Hooray! You've done good work! Now it's time to move those activity successes back to the goal sheets to see your actual progress on each of the individual goals.

While you're marking these activities as done on the goal sheets, count how many were completed for each goal this week. Fill in the number of completed activities in this week's column on the Goal Tracking Worksheet for each goal. While you're there, add the number of newly completed activities to the total completed so far at the end of last week. Put this number in the box for activities completed toward this goal so far.

If there are activities you had planned to do this week, but didn't get done, you can move them forward into the coming week. If there are some that simply take more

Find Your Meaning

Live the Stages

Getting Older

Identify Your Goals

Make Helpful Habits

Plan Your Days

Track Your Results

Practice Consistency

time than you expected, consider breaking them up into smaller pieces. Sometimes it's only when you start them that you find that some activities are too big to fit into a 2 hour time period.

See Your Weekly Accomplishments

When you've moved all the completed activities to their goal sheets and the Goal Tracking Worksheet, you can see how much you've accomplished. To see your whole week's productivity, total the number of completed activities for all goals this week, and put it in its line at the bottom. Then, to see your total completed activities so far, add this week's count to the number of activities completed so far from last week and put it into the total for this week so far. Congratulations on getting so much done!

See Your Habits Become Automatic

On the habit side of your To-Do list sheet, count the number of check marks in each habit row, and write the number next to the row of check marks. Then copy these numbers onto the Habit Tracking Worksheet in the habit column for this week.

How did you do? If most of the numbers in the column were 7, one for each day of the week, then your habits have become pretty regular. Congratulations! Keep up the good work.

If a few of the habits are less than 7, see how you've done on these habits in past weeks. If these habits have been consistently good, think about what could have gotten in the way this week. How could you keep this obstacle out of the way?

If some habits are consistently less than 7, they need a little investigation. What's keeping you from getting them done? Are they things you really want to happen? How can you bring your reasons for doing them to mind at the critical moment of action? Is there some preparation you can make to be sure that you're ready when the time for that habit comes?

Own and Celebrate Your Successes

In this culture, we tend to want to move right from one accomplishment to working on the next project. We often miss the chance to celebrate before we move on. Don't let it happen!

Look back over the activities of the past week and take credit for doing them. Share the news with your family. If you have grandchildren around, or even neighbor children, let them know about your projects and encourage them to give you a star or a sticker. Engaging them in your progress makes mutual encouragement a shared experience.

You can even encourage yourself by email. At the end of the day or week, you can send yourself a message with what you have done so far and what you plan to do next. It's a powerful way to have a record of your progress in your own words.

When you achieve a major goal, stop for a minute and savor the feeling of accomplishment. Remember what you wanted to achieve and why you wanted to achieve it. Look back at your goal description and remember why the goal was significant and why it mattered to you. Look at the things you had to do to get here and give yourself credit for the work and for the persistence to come through to the end. Notice how good you feel and remember the feeling. It will be one of the highlights you can come back to when you're in the middle of an effort that feels endless.

If you're one of those who are more motivated by rewards than punishments, find a reward to receive when you complete a goal. This could be anything from something big like a trip or buying a car you want to something more simple, such as treating yourself to a new outfit or a special meal. Rewards are powerful for motivating your inner child.

If you've promised yourself a reward for achieving this goal, collect on it! As you enjoy your treat, remember that you earned it. Enjoy not only the knowledge of your achievement, but also the awareness that you are competent and capable of making something you care about happen.

If you faced and overcame obstacles in the process, take a moment to think about the lessons you learned. Were there resources you turned to? Did you find help and support along the way? Were you surprised at yourself, either strengths you hadn't known about or weaknesses you hadn't anticipated? Record what you learned so that you'll have the benefit of this experience next time around.

Finally, don't forget to publicize your successes. Your friends and family care about you, and they're always happy to share a little good news. It doesn't have to sound like bragging; it can be as simple as letting folks know how happy you are about what you've accomplished. You might even add a little about what you hope to do next, just so you know there's an audience waiting for the next installment.

Find an Accountability Partner

Find someone you can talk with briefly—online or by phone—to help track your progress toward your goals. Make sure you choose a positive person who's willing to be helpful and encouraging. This is someone who will hold you to it when you aren't feeling energized or motivated. It could be a friend, partner, or family member.

Accountability partnerships involve regular checking in. For example, each morning, you hold a 5-minute phone call to share what you're committing to do that day. The next morning, you report on your progress from the previous day and share what you'll accomplish in the coming 24-hours. Knowing that your partner will be asking you whether you kept your commitments the day before can be a powerful motivator for getting tasks completed.

Better yet, find someone who has goals of their own and can use your input as they track their own progress. You can help each other find motivation, and by working

69

Find Your Meaning

Live the Stages

Getting Older

Identify Your Goals

Make Helpful Habits

Plan Your Days

Track Your Results

Practice Consistency

on a goal with someone else it means you have to show up for more than just yourself. You could even form an accountability group of folks who want to support and encourage each other as you work toward your goals together.

If you find that having a friend or colleague as your accountability partner isn't enough, consider hiring a professional, such as a coach or trainer. These folks may be better able to recognize self-sabotaging behaviors and beliefs – as well as to hold you accountable for taking action. If you're somebody who hates to waste money, knowing that you're paying someone to hold you accountable can be the extra motivation you need to help keep your commitments.

Goal Tracking Sample

○ Number of Activities Done This Week   □ Total Activities Done So Far

Goal	Week of:													
writing	○4 □4	○5 □9	○3 □12	○6 □18										
knitting			○2 □2	○2 □2										
medical	○2 □2	○1 □3	○3 □6	○2 □8										
fun	○3 □3	○4 □7	○2 □9	○3 □12										
family	○2 □2	○1 □3	○3 □6	○2 □8										
friends	○3 □3	○4 □7	○3 □10	○3 □13										
home	○2 □2	○3 □5	○2 □7	○3 □10										
faith	○1 □1	○2 □3	○1 □4	○2 □6										
Total for the Week:														

Find Your Meaning | Live the Stages | Getting Older | Identify Your Goals | Make Helpful Habits | Plan Your Days | Track Your Results | Practice Consistency

Habit Tracking Sample

Fill in the number of times each Habit was done this week.

Habit — Week of :	/	/	/	/	/	/	/	/	/	/
morning										
getting up routine	7	7	7	7						
exercise / physical therapy	6	5	7	6						
bath or shower	7	6	5	7						
dress	7	7	7	7						
breakfast	7	5	7	6						
consider purpose question	4	3	3	4						
review goals and direction	5	5	6	5						
day plan w/intentions	7	7	6	7						
set one unpleasant task first	5	5	4	5						
email / social media	7	7	7	7						
short local walk	3	4	2	5						
during the day										
exercise	5	5	5	5						
rest	4	6	3	7						
evening										
review goals and intentions	7	5	3	4						
tomorrow's plan list	7	7	7	7						
final email	7	7	7	7						
unwind (tv, knitting, ...)	7	7	7	7						
bath or shower		1	2							
undress for bed	7	7	7	7						
relax: tea / medication	5	6	5	6						
light reading / puzzles	3	5	4	6						
sleep	7	7	7	7						

Goal Tracking Worksheet

◯ Number of Activities Done This Week

☐ Total Activities Done So Far

Goal	Week of :	/	/	/	/	/	/	/	/	/	/	/	/

Total for the Week: _____

| Find Your Meaning | Live the Stages | Getting Older | Identify Your Goals | Make Helpful Habits | Plan Your Days | Track Your Results | Practice Consistency |

Habit Tracking Worksheet

Fill in the number of times each Habit was done this week.

Habit Week of :	/	/	/	/	/	/	/	/	/	/

morning

_____

_____

_____

_____

_____

_____

_____

_____

_____

_____

_____

_____

during the day

_____

_____

_____

_____

_____

_____

_____

evening

_____

_____

_____

_____

_____

_____

_____

_____

8. Practice Consistency and Flexibility

Find Your Meaning

Live the Stages

Getting Older

Identify Your Goals

Make Helpful Habits

Plan Your Days

Track Your Results

Practice Consistency

The purpose of the material in this workbook is to help you get control over the way you use your time and energy. The different suggestions are for you to use or not, as you see fit. Some ideas will work for you and some will not. Use what works and leave the rest behind.

My hope is to give you tools that will help you feel stronger and more confident in controlling your life. Please don't let anything that I've said lead you to create unrealistic expectations for yourself or to feel discouraged. What matters is only what you want to make with these tools. not what others do or say or expect or think.

This way of thinking about goals and directions isn't meant to be another taskmaster to take the place of the one you've left behind. It's only meant to help you find the goals and directions that belong to you, the things you want to do and the directions you want to go. It's meant to help you find your own path and to help you follow it effectively. It's meant to help you run your own life, not take it over and run it for you.

You can use the tools to discover what you want to do, and to do it. Try them out, see what you can do with them, and let go of whatever doesn't work for you.

Consistency, Persistence and Momentum

Consistency is a critically important factor in progress toward any goal. When you make a conscious decision to work towards a goal, you also need to make the decision to work consistently. This doesn't mean you have to do a lot of work every day just to reach your goal, but you do need to work on it frequently.

Consistently focusing attention towards your goals allows your brain to lock on to the target both consciously and unconsciously. When it comes to goals, consistency is the ability to keep up continuous effort despite whatever daily life brings against it. Consistency is essential in a task-orientated goal since it makes it possible for us to follow our results through to completion.

Consistency actually sharpens our minds. It creates powerful neural networks in the brain referred to as *grooving*. Grooved neural networks help form strong connections in the brain's synaptic connections, enhancing our ability to concentrate on a task or goal. When we only apply occasional effort toward a goal, the brain doesn't get enough stimuli to form powerful linkages. With consistent effort, our brain acquires these permanent neural connections as a result of our continuing activity.

Persistence is a state of mind, an indomitable will to succeed, based on connection with a persuasive "why?". Persistent people push through the setbacks and roadblocks that appear when we're moving ahead. Our ability to recover from failure and setbacks forms the basis for our future success.

Persistence recognizes that there really are external forces continually acting on us that have the potential to derail or hinder our progress. Persistent people recognize and take into account these forces working against them, but continue to make progress in spite of them. Persistent people show up with full attention, present and engaged with clear intention and purpose, whenever they focus on their goals.

Momentum then acts as an accelerator driving our persistence. As we maintain persistence, momentum takes the wheel to make progress feel normal and habitual. Once we're engaged and persistent, work on our goals takes on a life of its own, giving it extra energy as it moves forward.

Help Yourself Get Back on Track

It's normal to veer off course sometimes when we're pursuing our goals. Sometimes this happens because we're not fully committed to our goals. Other times, it's because we struggle to hold ourselves accountable for doing the necessary work. Sometimes it's a lack of resiliency, a failure in our ability to treat setbacks as part of the process that simply need to be overcome.

Here are a few techniques that you can use to get going again when you find that you've gotten off track.

Clarify Your Expectations

In order to be consistent and make progress, you have to remember what you want. Setting expectations will help you stay on track and remind you why you started on this journey in the first place. Telling yourself that you expect to succeed helps when negative thoughts appear. Counteract negatives with positive affirmations each time they come up. Reminding yourself what you're doing will push you through those tough spots.

The key here is to figure out how the thing you want to be consistent about makes you feel. Understanding your emotions about activities will help you stay focused and show up to do them on a regular basis.

If you feel like you're losing momentum toward your goals, you may need to verify your commitment. Sometimes our goals can be "should's," other people's expectations, rather than deep personal "want to's" that we want for ourselves. Without a burning desire to achieve a goal, our motivation can wane very quickly, and our subconscious mind turns its attention in other directions.

If this seems to be happening to you, take a look at your list of goals, and for each one ask, "What is my reason? Why do I want to achieve this? And am I committed enough to my why to do whatever it takes to achieve this goal?" By identifying or even upgrading your "why," you can tap into greater motivation and commitment to achieve your goal.

Remember the Big Picture

Step back and look at your work and your goal from the outside. Think about the accomplishments you've made so far. Look at the goal tracking sheets to be reminded of your progress. Go back to your original description of the goal. Focus on why it was important and why it particularly mattered to you. Remember the way you came to your strategy for achieving it.

Think about the work you've put in so far, and appreciate the effort. Then, cut yourself some slack. This goal is yours, not anybody else's hoop you have to jump through. Get rid of your self-criticism, any comparisons with the achievements of others, and any of the negative comments you heard somewhere back in childhood. The activities you're doing and the goal you're working toward are yours. You own it.

Refresh Your Feelings

Here is a little exercise to lift your spirits out of whatever doldrums they've fallen into. Take a few minutes for an attitude refresher:

- Take 3 deep breaths to calm yourself and relax.
- Notice your current mental and emotional state.
- Now recall a past accomplishment or a time when you overcame obstacles to reach a goal. Move into your memory to feel, really feel, and experience that moment. Enjoy your sense of mastery or achievement.
- Live in that feeling for a few minutes, and there you are!

When you focus on a feeling you've already experienced in the past, your brain actually starts feeling it again. To feel confident, just reflect on a time when you felt confident. It's almost like your brain needs to be reminded of what you're capable of doing.

This kind of exercise gives us a mental and emotional boost. It helps us forget about those feelings of inadequacy. If we use this activity regularly, we reinforce our belief that we can accomplish our goals.

Create Action Cues

An action cue is a tiny action plan that's been scientifically proven to help us follow through on our goals. An action cue is a basic if-then statement – if situation X arises, I will perform behavior Y. This kind of a statement would look like: "If it's 7:00am on Monday, Wednesday or Friday, I will go to the gym, and walk on the treadmill for 30 minutes." The key, of course, is to be so specific that you can't miss the cue when it happens, and you know exactly what you'll do next.

These techniques can help you re-engage with your goals when you've gotten distracted. You may be able to come up with other approaches that work for you.

Be Gentle with Yourself

When it comes to achieving goals, being perfect is not an option. Being perfect is not even a possibility. Consistency means working towards a goal more days than not, but it doesn't mean perfection. It's okay to miss a day. We're human and we're imperfect, so we can't expect our progress to be perfect.

Find Your Meaning

Live the Stages

Getting Older

Identify Your Goals

Make Helpful Habits

Plan Your Days

Track Your Results

Practice Consistency

Remember that consistency is key, so if you have a bad day, just try again the next day. If you slip ,just get back on track when you can, but don't see it as a failure. Progress is up and down, so remember that you won't always have great days.

At this stage of life, however, there's a distinction between laziness (and the need for discipline to get going) and a reasoned decision that the potential benefit of achieving a goal is not worth the cost to continue. There's no authority watching our goals or our target dates and giving us a grade for our success or failure. Our goals are set by our own choice, and we can change them or even remove them as we see fit.

If we find that a goal seems to be troublesome, this feeling is good information. If we're procrastinating about getting engaged in the activities, we need to think about why this is happening. Is the goal itself a "should" rather than truly a "want"? Are the activities harder than we thought they'd be? Is the goal downright unpleasant to work on? Do the activities just take much longer than we estimated?

If we like the goal but have trouble with the activities to get there, we can make changes. Is there an alternative approach that wouldn't require the problematic tasks? We can change the goal's plans. Are some of the activities harder than we expected? We can break them up into smaller units. Are there some activities we just can't do ourselves? We can add an activity to get someone else to do them.

What happens if the activities take longer than we thought? We can change the dates. If someone else is depending on us being done sooner than we can make happen, we can renegotiate the time frame, or help them find someone else to do our part. It's basic courtesy to let anyone depending on us know as soon as we do if we are not going to be able to honor our commitments.

At this stage of life, we have the experience to know that not all things are possible, and that there are some things that we simply can't do. Some solutions take longer to find than we have available, and some tasks aren't worth the cost to perform them. We've seen and we hopefully have learned to accept that not all problems have solutions. You don't have to take responsibility for what is not under your control.

The point of goal setting and tracking is not to force us to do the impossible or even the merely difficult. It's to help us do what we can do and want to do. We can only do what we can, and we can't do what we can't. Distinguishing between the two is known as wisdom.

We've been part of a culture that valued over-work, long days and long weeks in the workplace, with some extra work taken home as well. In retirement, hopefully this misplaced devotion to work has been left behind. There's no benefit to burning ourselves out in retirement, simply out of the habit of intensity. One joy of being in charge of our own goals and progress is that we can choose when to smile and walk away from any piece we choose to.

As you look at your progress, please don't forget to be gentle with yourself. We often have a habit of being stricter with ourselves than we are with others, and we usually don't even talk about it. Goal setting can sometimes lead us to high expectations of ourselves. Remember to forgive yourself for any and all apparent failings, real or imagined, that have become visible during these activities.

Go for It

As children of the sixties, we grew up believing we could change the world. Now as retirees, we can still change our corner of it for the better. I hold with the old saying, "Think globally, act locally." We can still work toward the ideals we've held, from whatever place and with whatever time and energy we have to use.

The world still needs what we can contribute, both in our immediate world of friends and family and in the wider world. You alone know what matters to you and how you can make your own difference. I encourage you to use these ideas to make every moment count.

Made in the USA
Columbia, SC
02 January 2018